Quick
A Journey
Through the Bible

AN 8-PART INTRODUCTION TO THE BIBLE TIMELINE

LEADER'S GUIDE

SARAH CHRISTMYER

ASCENSION PRESS

West Chester, Pennsylvania

Nihil obstat: Msgr. Joseph G. Prior, SSL, STD
Censor Librorum
June 3, 2008

Imprimatur: +Justin Cardinal Rigali
Archbishop of Philadelphia
June 9, 2008

A Quick Journey Through the Bible: An Eight-Part Introduction to The Bible Timeline is a resource of *The Great Adventure* Bible Study Program.

Jeff Cavins, General Editor, *The Great Adventure* Bible Study Program
Sarah Christmyer, Editor, *The Great Adventure* Bible Study Program, and Author, *A Quick Journey Through the Bible*

Scripture verses contained herein are from the Catholic Edition of the Revised Standard Version of the Bible, copyright 1965, 1966 by the Division of Christian Education of the National Council of Churches of Christ in the United States of America. Used by permission.

Ascension Press
Post Office Box 1990
West Chester, PA 19380
Orders: 1-800-376-0520
AscensionPress.com
BibleStudyforCatholics.com

Printed in the United States of America

ISBN 978-1-934217-12-2

CONTENTS

Leader's Introduction iii

Welcome to *The Great Adventure!*. xi

About *The Great Adventure: A Journey through the Bible* xii

Frequently-Asked Questions (FAQs) xiii

    1. Which Bible should I use?

    2. How do I find a reference in my Bible?

    3. What is the Bible?

    4. Why are Catholic and a Protestant Bibles different?

Session 1: *Introduction* 1

Session 2: *Early World* 7

Session 3: *Patriarchs* 11

    Covenantal Structure of Salvation History 12

    Map of Abraham's Journey 13

Session 4: *Egypt and Exodus, Desert Wanderings* 17

    The Route of the Exodus 18

    The Plan of the Tabernacle 18

    Map of the Conquest of Canaan 22

    Map of Israel: the Twelve Tribes 22

Session 5: *Conquest and Judges, Royal Kingdom* 23

    Map of the Divided Kingdom 28

Session 6: *Divided Kingdom, Exile* 29

    Kings of Israel and Judah 34

    Prophets of the Northern and Southern Kingdoms 36

Session 7: *Return, Maccabean Revolt* 37

Session 8: *Messianic Fulfillment, The Church* 43

Responsive Prayer 46

Continuing the Journey 47

Reading Through the Bible Historically: 90-Day Reading Plan 48

Chart of Narrative and Supplemental Books 49

Books of Bible -

Leader's Introduction

Background and Course Description

The Great Adventure is a Catholic Bible study program that teaches God's plan of salvation as it unfolds in Scripture, presented from within the living Tradition of the Catholic Church. Through parish Bible studies and resources, seminars, and conferences, *The Great Adventure* helps people read "the big picture" of God's plan in Scripture; find their place in that story; and live it out in their lives.

In *A Quick Journey through the Bible*, Jeff Cavins presents an introduction to *The Bible Timeline*: a chronological presentation of the key people and events in the Bible, divided into time periods and color-coded to help people remember the flow. Eight, half-hour talks convey the story and explain how that inspired narrative, read from within the heart of the Catholic Church, unlocks the meaning of our faith.

By the end of this program, participants should be able to:

- Recall the progression of the story of salvation history

- Recognize how God's plan unfolded through a series of covenant promises made with His people

- Use the full-color *Bible Timeline* chart or bookmark to place any Bible reading within the context of the overall Bible narrative

Most importantly, students should begin reading Scripture and hearing the readings at Mass with a new and deeper understanding.

The Goal of *The Great Adventure*

The primary goal of *The Great Adventure* is simply to introduce Catholics to Scripture and to make the Bible approachable by explaining the overarching story and showing how the various books fit together to get that story across. We believe that once people understand the "narrative thread" of the entire story, they are far better prepared to understand not just the individual parts, but also more complicated matters related to the Christian faith. Therefore, the program focuses first and foremost on the final form of the text, using what is often referred to as the canonical or narrative approach to Scripture. This approach is common throughout the Catholic tradition (see, for example, the *Didascalicon* of Hugh of St. Victor, Book 6, Chapter 3, or observations in the Pontifical Biblical Commission's *The Interpretation of the Bible in the Church*, 1993). It also fits into the criteria for interpreting Scripture laid out in the Vatican II document *Dei Verbum* and explained in the *Catechism of the Catholic Church* (CCC), which says to "be especially attentive 'to the content and unity of the whole Scripture' (DV 12) ... Scripture is a unity by reason of the unity of God's plan" (CCC 112). It is that plan which *The Great Adventure* seeks to get across.

Course Outline

Session #	Title	Narrative Book
Session 1	Introduction	—
Session 2	Early World	Genesis 1-11
Session 3	Patriarchs	Genesis 12-50
Session 4	Egypt and Exodus Desert Wanderings	Exodus Numbers
Session 5	Conquest and Judges Royal Kingdom	Joshua, Judges 1,2 Samuel, 1 Kings 1-11
Session 6	Divided Kingdom Exile	1 Kings 12-22, 2 Kings 2 Kings 17, 25
Session 7	Return Maccabean Revolt	Ezra, Nehemiah 1 Maccabees
Session 8	Messianic Fulfillment The Church	Luke Acts

Materials

Lecture Set (available on DVD and CD)

Jeff Cavins explains the *Bible Timeline* and the twelve periods of Bible history in a series of eight, half-hour talks called *A Quick Journey Through the Bible*. The same series was previously sold under the titles *The Great Adventure Eight-Week Course* and the *Bible Timeline Seminar Eight-Week Course*.

Student Workbook (one per student)

Each Student Workbook contains an introduction to the program; helpful maps and charts; talk outlines with room for taking notes; questions for class discussion; and an optional assignment for home preparation. Included with each workbook are the following collateral materials:

- *The Bible Timeline* **chart**: A full-color timeline of salvation history that places the key people and events of salvation history in chronological order and divides them into twelve historical periods. A color-coded system is used as a memory aid. The chart illustrates which books of the Bible narrate the story and how the rest fit into the historic framework; highlights the major covenants by which God formed His family on Earth; and indicates major events in secular history for each time period. Christ's bloodline is traced, beginning with Adam. Folds to fit into a Bible.

- *The Bible Timeline* **bookmark**: This quick-reference guide to *The Bible Timeline* periods helps you identify the books of the Bible that tell each stage of the story at a glance. It also illustrates the placement of the remaining books and describes the meanings of the period colors.

- *The Bible Timeline* **memory bead wristband**: Twelve colored beads corresponding to the colors assigned to the twelve time periods and strung on a leather wristband form a unique aid to learning the framework of Bible history.

Leader's Guide (one per leader)

The Leader's Guide, which contains the full text of the Student Workbook, explains *A Quick Journey* and gives suggestions for organizing the class as well as guidelines for facilitating in-class discussion and answering the discussion questions.

The Bible (all participants)

For recommendations regarding which version to use, see the Frequently-Asked Questions section of the workbook. A Catholic version is required.

Preparing to Lead *A Quick Journey Through the Bible*

1) Thoroughly familiarize yourself with all the course materials before you begin.

2) Register on the Leader's Portal of BibleStudyforCatholics.com for help with running your study.

3) Schedule eight sessions of ninety minutes each.

4) Limit discussion groups to twelve people each for best results. Identify several group leaders ahead of time so you can break into smaller groups after listening to the talk.

5) The person or people facilitating the group discussion should view each week's talk, do the preparation exercises, and review the discussion guide in advance of each class. See "Guide for Group Facilitators" on page vii.

How to Structure the Class

Allow ninety minutes for each class to give time for people to gather and break into/return from small groups. An agenda that includes an introduction, lecture, discussion, and closing is explained below.

STEP 1: Introduction (fifteen minutes)
      –Welcome and Prayer
      –Opening Review

The first week, spend this opening time distributing and explaining materials and telling students what to expect. There is time during the discussion period for people in small groups to begin getting to know one another.

Begin each subsequent week with a brief review of the previous lesson or of the story thus far. This is a good time to have people practice learning the period colors using their memory bead wristbands. As time goes on, make it a contest. How many people can recite the whole string? Now and then you might have people take out their charts so you can test them: can they tell you which narrative books are in the time of the Royal Kingdom? Who in Jesus' ancestry is in the time of the Patriarchs? Can anyone give you a one-sentence description of the period you just finished? And so on.

Introduce the name and color of the new period(s) before you show the DVD. Suggestions specific to each lesson can be found in the Leader's Notes at the start of each lesson.

STEP 2: View DVD (thirty minutes)
The teaching tapes for *A Quick Journey Through the Bible* are also available on CD.

STEP 3: Small group discussion (forty minutes)
To make the most of the discussion, limit your group to eight to twelve people. It is very important to keep the discussion on topic or the material may not all be covered. This is the job of the leader—along with encouraging participation, drawing out answers, and keeping one person from dominating the discussion. The facilitator should answer a question only if no one else can answer. When possible, he or she should attempt to point the participants toward the response instead of giving it directly. Difficult questions can be addressed later (the leader should determine in advance the best way to handle such questions so he or she can keep the group running smoothly).

Responses to the questions are printed on the pages facing the questions in the Leader's Guide.

STEP 4: Closing (five minutes)
If there are several small groups in your class, you might consider gathering together at the end and having each group share one thing they learned.

Close all but the first lesson with a responsive reading of the prayer printed on page 46 of the Student Workbook. The leader can read the first line pertaining to each period, or group members can take turns. Read up through the period which you have just learned about.

Alternately, you may choose to pray just the piece related to the period you are studying. These are written into Step 4 under "Prayer" at the end of each lesson.

The Role of the Home Study Questions

A Home Study section at the close of each lesson is provided to help students prepare for the following week. That preparation is done in two parts: first, basic information is gleaned about the coming time period from the *Bible Timeline* chart. Second, key passages from the book of the Bible that tell the story of that period are listed. Encourage participants to read at least some of these passages, as they will hear about in the following lecture.

It's time to begin! Please read all leader's information carefully and view Jeff Cavins' lecture before leading each lesson.

Guide for Group Facilitators

A facilitator is NOT a catechist, theologian, or counselor. The facilitator's job is not to teach, advise, or even to answer questions, but rather to welcome group members and guide them through the lesson, aiming to give everyone a chance to participate.

The facilitator does not make a discussion good;
he or she makes a good discussion possible.

A *Quick Journey through the Bible* will take your group on a fast-paced journey through the entire story of salvation as it unfolds in the Bible, from Creation and the Fall through the coming of Christ and the establishment of the Church. On the way, you'll catch a glimpse of fascinating people and events and you'll begin to see how knowing that story helps you understand your faith. It seems counter-intuitive, but stopping to dig in deeper before you get that big picture can work against the goal of the program, which is simply to lay out the underlying narrative in order to provide a context for later exploration. As a facilitator, it will be your job to help your group stay focused on the larger goal.

You may want to read these words to your group the first week, and refer to them from time to time. They are taken from the introduction to *The Bible Timeline Guided Journal*, in the section "Staying Focused":

> One of the hardest things to do when you are reading through the Bible to get an overview of the story is to stay focused. You are bound to run into things you don't understand or things you want to know more about. If you read with the goal of taking it all in at once or of understanding everything, you will be frustrated. It may help to remember these things:
>
> You have the rest of your life to get the details. This is not just any book, it is the Word of God. The Bible has proved to be deep and rich enough to keep some of the world's best minds going for a lifetime.
>
> It's OK to have questions. Remember that getting the big picture up front will help you make sense of the pieces later on. Having questions will also keep you coming back for more. [...]
>
> One way to think about what you are doing is to consider the way an artist paints a mural. He or she never starts on one side and paints across to the other. Rather, they first chalk out the main lines of the composition, then paint a very pale "under-painting" of several colors over the whole thing. It doesn't look good, but that doesn't matter: its purpose it to lay a foundation for the rest. Next the mid-tones go on, then the shadows and finally the highlights. To apply this to *The Bible Timeline*, the [*Quick Journey*] chalks out the main lines of the composition: the 12 periods, the people and events. Your first read-through provides the under-painting. Mid-tones and shadows and highlights will come as you read more and study. The "painting"—your under-standing of Scripture—will get more and more detailed as time goes on.
>
> If you forget this and get frustrated as you read, you are not alone. It's human nature to want to understand. But none of us will ever get to the end of the Bible. That's the

beauty of it! So sit back, and try to get that under-painting done. It may not be pretty, but it will help form a good foundation for the reading you do for the rest of your life.[1]

Some additional tips follow:

Tip #1: Be prepared

- Go to the Leader's Portal and Your Study World on www.BibleStudyforCatholics.com to read tips appropriate to each particular session.

- Read the entire lesson in the workbook ahead of time and do any recommended exercises and readings. Pay particular attention to the facilitator instructions and responses on the left-hand pages of the workbook, opposite the discussion questions.

- Discussion questions for *A Quick Journey through the Bible* are based on the DVD lesson people view during the class time. If you are facilitating a *Quick Journey* discussion, it will be helpful to view the DVD in advance. If you can't, take particular care to review the discussion questions and responses in advance. As you watch the DVD during the class time, jot down things you want to remember or draw attention to during the discussion.

Tip #2: Set the tone: act as a host

- Be welcoming and enthusiastic.

- Good hosts look out for the needs of their guests before their own. Resist the temptation to answer or comment on every question, and draw the others out instead.

Tip #3: Lead the way: act as a trail guide

- Take control. You are the leader; the group will expect you to move them along and keep them on track.

- Start on time, every time. Assign a member of your group to watch the clock and warn you when you near the end of the allotted time.

- Prepare ahead of time ways to encourage discussion and reflection on the DVD, especially if your group is quiet.

Tip #4: Encourage others: act as a cheerleader

- Watch for clues that a more reserved person has something to say and encourage them without putting them on the spot.

---

[1] Sarah Christmyer, *The Bible Timeline Guided Journal* (West Chester, PA: Ascension Press, 2007), xii.

- If you have extra group time, have fun with it: use the colored beads and the prayer to help people learn the 12 periods and highlights of each. Pose a challenge among the groups, to see which can learn them first in order, or identify the key people or events, etc. Ask what struck them personally in the reading they did, or what new they learned from the video. Focus on things they learned, not things they don't know (there will always be plenty of these!)

- Don't be afraid of silence. If it continues too long (try praying a Hail Mary or Our Father silently while you wait), you may find it helpful to answer the first part of a long question yourself, and then re-phrase the question to draw out the rest. Try not to answer the whole thing for them.

Tip #5: Direct the discussion: act as a traffic cop

- Prepare ways to kindly curb someone who dominates the group, to give others a chance to speak. If they continue, ask privately if they will help you get others to participate.

- Gently re-direct tangents ("That's an interesting point, John, thank you for sharing. Now to get back to the questions—did anyone have anything else to add before we move on?").

- Use body language to reinforce your message: thank someone for their insight, then turn your body toward another, physically indicating a stop in that "traffic" and a green light for others.

- **Handling Tough Questions:** It is common for people who are new to Scripture to go beyond the lessons in the *Quick Journey* workbook and throw out theological questions that have bothered them for years. Remember that a facilitator is not a teacher. At no time should you feel that you must be able to answer additional questions that arise, particularly difficult theological questions. It is okay to simply say, "That is an interesting question! I wish I could answer it, but we're getting off topic and I need to move us on now."

  As much as you may want to answer all of their questions (and unless there is someone present who has the time and who is able to properly answer), these questions are best handled in a different setting. If you plan to offer *The Bible Timeline: the Story of Salvation* as a follow-up to the *Quick Journey*, you can ask people to keep track of their questions until they do that deeper study of the Bible.

Tip #6: "Let go, and let God"

- Prepare, pay attention, do your best, pray for God's help - and then enjoy hearing what everyone brings up from their experience.

Ten Commandments of a Small Group

I. Be prepared

II. Come on time

III. If you did not prepare, allow others to speak before you do

IV. Listen to others

V. Stick to the topic and questions at hand

VI. Never ridicule or cut down another's answer

VII. When you disagree, do so with respect and charity

VIII. Don't fear silence

IX. Don't share confidences outside the group

X. Enjoy yourself!

Alphabetical "Rules of the Road"

- Be **A**udible,

- Be **B**rief,

- Be **C**hrist-**C**entered; and

- **D**on't **D**ouble-**D**ip! (give your input, then allow others to speak)

The following four pages are reprinted from the opening pages of the Student Workbook. The page numbers in the Student Workbook are pp. v-viii.

WELCOME TO THE GREAT ADVENTURE!

Pope Benedict XVI, as Joseph Cardinal Ratzinger, wrote that "God created the universe in order to enter into a history of love with humankind."[1]

Not just a *relationship* of love; a *history* of love.

There is a difference. Lots of people fall in love. Lots of people are "in a relationship." But lots of those relationships fall apart. There are many reasons why the ones that last do, but one of them has to be that the couples didn't stop with a surface relationship. They know each others' histories, where they come from and where they are going. Not only that, they have *entered into* each others' histories in such a way that they now *share a story*. They have entered, you might say, a joint "history of love." There exists between them a depth and intimacy of knowing that is impossible to attain otherwise.

The beginnings of that history of love are recorded in Sacred Scripture, and this history continues today in the life of the Church. Each of us is called by God to enter into that history. But if I do not know that history, even in the broadest outline, if my faith is centered merely on myself and God right now when I need Him, I am going to have a hard time *entering* into that history the way God has created me to. I will have a difficult time understanding Him when He speaks to me through the Scriptures. I will find it difficult to know things such as why the sacraments are important or what role the Church plays in the overall scheme of things. I will find it hard to attain to the great depth and intimacy of knowing and loving God to which I am called.

As St. Augustine has said, "To fall in love with God is the greatest of all romances; to seek Him, the greatest adventure..." What we offer in *The Great Adventure* is a way to seek God by learning that "history of love" (i.e., the narrative thread that is found in Scripture) and by discovering where your life fits into the Story.

Whether you are new to Scripture study or have been reading it all your life, we hope and pray that this *Quick Journey Through the Bible* starts you off on a lifelong adventure of getting to know God in His written word.

---

[1] Pope Benedict XVI (Joseph Cardinal Ratzinger), *"In the Beginning…" A Catholic Understanding of the Story of Creation and the Fall* (Grand Rapids, MI: William B. Eerdmans, 1995), translated by Boniface Ramsay, OP, p. 30.

Before you begin your study, visit **BibleStudyforCatholics.com**, click on the "Students" link, and sign up for "Your Study World."

Here, you can track your weekly reading assignment progress and get helpful tips and words of encouragement as you progress through the study.

ABOUT THE GREAT ADVENTURE: A JOURNEY THROUGH THE BIBLE

Jeff Cavins developed *The Great Adventure: A Journey Thorugh the Bible* in 1984 when he realized that many Christians did not grasp "the big picture" of the Scriptures. Though people knew selected stories, they were not able to connect them into a full narrative. His answer was to identify the books of the Bible that tell the story from beginning to end. By reading just these fourteen "narrative" books, a chronological story emerges. From this idea grew the immensely popular *Bible Timeline Seminar*: a day-long program that teaches the story in a way that is easy to remember and helps people to continue reading Scripture on their own. Hundreds of thousands of people have learned to read the Bible with the help of this system.

In 2002, Jeff joined with Sarah Christmyer, Dr. Timothy Gray, and Ascension Press to take the narrative approach to reading Scripture that characterizes the *Bible Timeline Seminar* and develop it into a comprehensive program to help Catholics learn to read and study the Bible in the light of the Church. Since then, a number of programs have been developed to expand upon the original seminar. First, *A Quick Journey through the Bible* takes the basic seminar material and spreads it over eight sessions.

A combination of eight, half-hour lectures and materials for light home study help the student get a better grasp of the story than is sometimes possible from the seminar alone.

A new *Guided Journal* walks readers through the *Bible Timeline* reading plan. This is a good way to learn the story of Scripture firsthand while reinforcing lessons learned in the Seminar. It is also excellent preparation for doing *The Bible Timeline: The Story of Salvation*. This 24-part course is the first step in a foundational Bible study series, so called because together the studies establish a basic foundation of Bible knowledge that forms an ideal platform for continued reading and study. Step Two, *Matthew: the King and His Kingdom,* focuses on Jesus as the fulfillment of the promises of the Old Testament. It also touches on Jesus' establishment of the Church, which is the Kingdom of Heaven on Earth. Building on those studies is Step Three, *Acts: The Spread of the Kingdom.* This shows how Christ's work continues through each of us in the Church today. Studies on other books of the Bible round out the program.

FREQUENTLY-ASKED QUESTIONS

1. Which Bible should I use?

For this study, you will want to use a Catholic Bible such as:

- *Revised Standard Version—Catholic Edition (RSV-CE)*: a literal translation recommended for serious Bible study. This version is cited in the *Catechism of the Catholic Church* and is referenced in all *Bible Timeline* materials.

- *New American Bible (NAB)*: a more "dynamic" translation that strives for greater readability; used in the liturgy.

- *New Jerusalem Bible (NJB)*: a "dynamic equivalent" version that is less literal yet still faithful to the original meaning.

- *The Way—The Catholic Living Bible*: written in modern, easy-to-understand language. Useful for beginners who want to read the Story, but a more literal translation is preferred for actual study.

2. How do I find a Scripture reference in my Bible?

Each book of the Bible is divided into chapters, and each chapter is made up of a series of numbered verses. To aid readers in finding a particular biblical verse, each Scripture passage has an "address": a location reference made up of the name of the book, followed by the chapter and verse numbers. For example:

- *1 Samuel 7* refers to the entire seventh chapter of the book of 1 Samuel (pronounced "first Samuel" because there also is a 2 Samuel, or "second Samuel").

- *Genesis 1:1* refers to the book of Genesis, chapter 1, verse 1.

- *Numbers 5:2–6* refers to the book of Numbers, chapter 5, verses 2, 3, 4, 5, and 6, i.e., consecutive verses.

- *1 Corinthians 3:2–6, 7-10* refers to the book of 1 Corinthians, chapter 3, verses 2 through 6 and verses 7 through 10.

Abbreviations are often used in Scripture references. For example, "Jn 3:16" means "John, chapter 3, verse 16." A list of abbreviations is found in the front of your Bible. To locate a particular book, use your Bible's table of contents.

3. What is the Bible?

The Bible is a collection of seventy-three books. Some are historical; others are poetic or prophetic, or are what is called wisdom literature. They were written by many authors over many years and in several languages. They are grouped under two headings: the Old Testament and the New Testament. The word for "testament" can also be translated "covenant"—a word choice that clarifies the meaning of the titles "Old" and "New Testament." The Old Testament tells how God made a series of *covenants* (binding agreements) with what became the nation of Israel in which He promised blessing and membership in His family in return for loving obedience. The New Testament tells how God fulfilled those promises by means of a *new covenant* in His son Jesus Christ.

What Christians call the Old Testament was originally the Hebrew canon of scripture. Today the Jewish canon contains thirty-nine books of three different types:

- **The Law** (Torah), also called the Pentateuch or the Books of Moses: Genesis, Exodus, Leviticus, Numbers, Deuteronomy.

- **The Prophets**: Joshua, Judges, 1st and 2nd Samuel, 1st and 2nd Kings, Isaiah, Jeremiah, Ezekiel, Hosea, Joel, Amos, Obadiah, Jonah,

Micah, Nahum, Habakkuk, Zephaniah, Haggai, Zechariah, Malachi.

- **The Writings**: Psalms, Proverbs, Job, Song of Songs, Ruth, Lamentations, Ecclesiastes, Esther, Daniel, Ezra-Nehemiah, 1st and 2nd Chronicles.

4. Why are Catholic and Protestant Bibles different?

The earliest Christians spoke Greek and used a Greek translation of the Hebrew Scriptures called the *Septuagint*. This included the thirty-nine books named above plus seven books that Jews today consider sacred but do not include in their canon: Tobit, Judith, 1 and 2 Maccabees, Wisdom, Ecclesiasticus (aka Sirach), Baruch, and some additional passages in Daniel and Esther. Roman Catholic Bibles follow the early Christians and include all forty-six books in their Old Testament. At the time of the Reformation, the Protestant Reformers chose to follow the shorter Hebrew canon.

All Christians, whether Catholic or Protestant, include the same twenty-seven books in the New Testament. It contains several types of books:

- **The Gospels and Acts of the Apostles**: Matthew, Mark, Luke, John, and Acts.

- **Paul's Letters to the Churches**: Romans, 1 and 2 Corinthians, Galatians, Ephesians, Philippians, Colossians, 1st and 2nd Thessalonians.

- **The Pastoral Letters**: 1st and 2nd Timothy, Titus, Philemon, Hebrews.

- **The Catholic Letters and the Book of Revelation**: James, 1st and 2nd Peter, 1st, 2nd, and 3rd John, Jude, and Revelation.

From this point on, information for leaders is printed on the left page, opposite the page from the Student Workbook to which it refers. All the pages from the Student Workbook have been reproduced on the right. The page numbers are the same in both workbooks for ease of reference.

Take advantage of the many resources offered on The Great Adventure website (www. BibleStudyforCatholics.com) to help you organize, run, and publicize this and other Great Adventure Bible studies. Once you have set a start date for your study, sign up for "Your Study World" on the website for practical tips related to each session of A Quick Journey Through the Bible. Participants in your group can also sign up as students to access words of encouragement and hints for getting the most from their study.

PREPARING TO LEAD SESSION 1: INTRODUCTION

- For this session only, read all instructions to leaders, preview the DVD, and familiarize yourself with all questions and responses.

- Carefully read the following Lesson Overview:

Lesson Overview

In Session 1, Jeff Cavins introduces The Bible Timeline by explaining the importance of Scripture in the Catholic faith and then looking at why many Catholics find it so hard to read the Bible. The Church's solution, he says, can be found in the structure of the Catechism of the Catholic Church (CCC), which starts with, and builds everything else on, the Creed. The Creed can be thought of as the story of salvation history "in tightly wound form," and it is this story that makes sense of all things Catholic. Finally, Jeff explains how to find that story in Scripture by using The Bible Timeline.

The Bible Timeline learning system makes the complex simple by isolating the key people and events in the Bible and arranging them on a chronological timeline. It then identifies fourteen narrative books (out of seventy-three total books) of the Bible: the fourteen books that, read in order, tell the story from start to finish. These books are arranged across the timeline and then the whole thing is divided into twelve distinct periods and color-coded as a memory aid. Make sure you understand this system and how to read the Bible Timeline chart before offering this introductory session.

In subsequent lessons, Jeff will go through each of the twelve periods in order as he tells the story. Class discussion and home preparation will reinforce the lessons and help participants get familiar with reading the Bible.

LEADING THE CLASS SESSION

STEP 1 – Opening Review (fifteen minutes)
- Use the information provided in the Lesson Overview above to tell participants what to expect from this lesson.
- Distribute and explain the materials. Make sure everyone has a workbook, chart, bookmark, and memory bead wristband.
- Point out the introductory material at the front of the Student Workbook, including the Frequently-Asked Questions section. If people in your group are very new to the Bible, you may want to go over these questions with them. Explain that class time will be divided between a talk and small group discussion.
- If your group is not too large, you might ask each person to introduce themselves and tell what they hope to get out of the class. You may need to spend more than fifteen minutes doing the Opening Review this first session. If so, you may take time from the group discussion to make up for it and leave some of those questions to be done at home.

STEP 2 – View DVD (thirty minutes)
The Student Workbook section for each lesson begins with a brief outline of Jeff Cavins' talk. Space is included in that outline (see facing page) for taking notes. Ask group members to write down at least one thing that stands out to them from the talk to share later with the class.

NOTES

1. Scripture in the Catholic Church

2. The Problem

   Magisterium (teacher)
   Inspired – Spirit(ed)

3. The Church's Solution: Start with the Story

   • The Creed

   • Sacraments and Liturgy

   • Life in Christ

   • Prayer

4. Finding the story in Scripture

1. Answers will vary; encourage discussion. Skip this question if you discussed it during the opening.

2. The Church fathers followed a narrative approach to teaching catechumens in which their explanation of the Christian faith was built upon the story of God's working with His people as it is told in the Bible. The *Catechism of the Catholic Church*, which you might think of as containing all that is in that "heap of Catholicism," reflects this in its structure. All the information in the "heap" has been sorted into four "pillars":

    i. <u>The Creed</u>, as St. Augustine tells us, is the story of salvation history "in tightly wound form." It comes first for a reason. Pillars 2 through 4 spring from the story that is told in the Bible.

    ii. <u>Sacraments and Liturgy</u> comes next. They are how you get into the Story.

    iii. <u>Life in Christ</u> is where you find your place in the Story. It is your personal script for living it.

    iv. <u>Prayer</u> is the final pillar. It is where intimacy with God develops, the goal of the Story.

3. Each book of the Bible is linked to the other books by the "narrative thread" of God's plan. If you don't know that plan (which includes things like why we are here, and what went wrong at the beginning, and how God set about making things right again) it will be very hard to make sense of the various parts.

    Another reason to learn the whole picture is that from the very beginning, God taught His people to pass down the Story of all He had done for them. As the story continues, they refer back to past events and look forward to things that have been promised. If you enter in the middle of the story, there will be many references you do not understand. The gospels, with which most Catholics are very familiar, are full of references to the Old Testament. Reading without an understanding of these things, it is impossible to comprehend the intended meaning of the text. Consequently, the *Catechism* tells us that in interpreting Scripture it is essential to be "attentive to the content and unity of the whole Scripture" (*CCC* 112) and to "the way the truths of faith hang together among themselves and within the whole plan of divine Revelation" (*CCC* 114).

After discussing questions 1–3, read the paragraphs that follow them on the student page and have participants follow the instructions. The story outline that follows will briefly introduce them to the twelve periods of salvation history and to the color-coding system utilized by The Bible Timeline.

DISCUSSION QUESTIONS

1. Several common difficulties people have when they start to read the Bible were mentioned in the lecture. What has been your experience with Scripture?

2. Many Catholics today feel as though they have received a "heap of Catholicism," a random pile of separate Bible stories and facts about what the Church teaches. What solution do the four "pillars" of the *Catechism* present to this problem?

3. Why is it important to get the "big picture" of salvation history before reading or studying the Bible?

The stories in the Old and New Testaments are not disconnected, random events in the history of a people. Rather, each one is a crucial part of God's plan. By the end of this course, you will see the narrative thread that runs throughout Scripture and continues in your life today.

The Bible Timeline chart groups the stories into twelve consecutive historical periods that are color-coded to help you remember them. Look at each period on the chart (or follow along on your memory bead wristband) while someone reads the story in outline form as follows:

- In the **Early World**, God created the heavens and earth and tested Adam and Eve in the garden. This period is represented by the color **turquoise**, which is the color of the earth seen from space.

- In the time of the **Patriarchs**, God called Abraham and promised his children land, a royal kingdom, and world-wide blessing. The color **burgundy** helps us remember the blood covenant God made with him.

- In **Egypt and Exodus**, God freed His people from slavery so they could worship Him. **Red** reminds us of the crossing of the Red Sea.

- God taught Israel to trust Him through forty years of **Desert Wanderings**. What better way to remember those miles of sand than by the color **tan**?

Questions 4–8 introduce and explain the various features of The Bible Timeline *chart. If you do not have time to cover them in class, you may leave any remaining questions to be done with the questions for home study.*

4. The fourteen narrative books and the periods of salvation that they describe are: Genesis 1-11 (Early World), Genesis 12-50 (Patriarchs), Exodus (Egypt and Exodus), Numbers (Desert Wanderings), Joshua and Judges (Conquest and Judges), 1 and 2 Samuel, 1 Kings 1-11 (Royal Kingdom), 1 Kings 12-22, 2 Kings (Divided Kingdom), 2 Kings 17, 25 (Exile), Ezra and Nehemiah (Return), 1 Maccabees (Maccabean Revolt), Luke (Messianic Fulfillment), and Acts of the Apostles (The Church).

- In **Conquest and Judges**, God led Israel triumphantly in the Promised Land, represented by **green** for the lush hills of Canaan.

- There He established Israel as a **Royal Kingdom** under David, who was promised an eternal throne. The color **purple** represents the royal throne.

- Israel soon split into rival kingdoms and fell into idolatry. **Black** represents the darkness of this **Divided Kingdom**.

- God punished both kingdoms with **Exile**; **baby blue** recalls the children of Judah "singing the blues" in Babylon.

- Brighter days of **Return** are shown by **yellow**: God brought the exiles home to make a fresh start.

- Years later, the Maccabees stood up against the threats of Hellenization in the **Maccabean Revolt**. The color **orange** calls to mind the lit oil lamps in the purified Temple.

- **Gold** represents the first New Testament period, the time of **Messianic Fulfillment**: when God at last sent His only son, Jesus Christ the Messiah, to fulfill all His promises. Remember gold by the gifts of the Magi.

- Finally, **the Church** carries on God's work in the world. Its color is **white**, for the spotless Bride of Christ.

4. The "narrative books" section gives you the names of fourteen books of the Bible that tell the Story from beginning to end. They are arranged across the top of the chart so you can see what historical time period(s) they describe. What are they?

5. 1 and 2 Chronicles provide a parallel historical account of the time. The so-called "wisdom literature" was also written: Psalms, Proverbs, Ecclesiastes, and Song of Solomon. Many of these were written by one of the two primary kings of the Royal Kingdom: David and Solomon.

6. The family group grows from One Holy Couple (Adam and Eve) to One Holy Family (Noah, his wife and sons) in the Early World, to One Holy Tribe (under Abraham) in the time of the Patriarchs, to One Holy Nation (under Moses) after the Exodus, to One Holy Kingdom (under David) in Royal Kingdom, and finally One Holy Catholic and Apostolic Church (in the new covenant with Jesus Christ). The thing to notice is that it grows! God started with a couple and built, over time, a world-wide family with membership in the kingdom of God.

7. *Understanding the Bible Timeline Chart* is a full-color guide sheet that is included in both the Leader's and Student's Packs.

    Hint: Look for the big arrows that point from one horizontal section to another and for other times the bloodline crosses between areas. The major movements are:

    1) God calls Abram out of Ur (Event No. 6; from the Northern countries into the land of Canaan; beginning of the Patriarchs period). There is another minor move during this time when Jacob flees into the North and has his sons.

    2) Jacob's family moves to Egypt (Event No. 14; from Canaan into South and Egypt at the close of the Patriarchs).

    3) Israel's move from the Egypt to Canaan across the Desert Wanderings period (there is no arrow).

    4) Israel goes into Assyrian exile and Judah falls to Babylon (Event Nos. 44 and 47; four arrows in Exile period).

    5) Three returns to Canaan in the Return.

8. Answers will vary with the periods people select. If there is time, allow some discussion of this. It is important for people to know and understand that biblical history is written about real people to whom real things happened in real time, in countries that we know about already. As the weeks go on, it will become clear that you cannot study the Bible in a vacuum. The situations in the surrounding countries have a dramatic impact on the Bible story.

5. Fifty-nine "supplemental books" make up the rest of the Bible. These are not any less important than the "narrative books," but for our purposes we will set them aside. Once you have learned the chronological story told in the narrative books, you will want to check the chart to see where the remaining books fit into that historical context before you read them.

   Look at the top of the purple Royal Kingdom period. 1 and 2 Samuel and 1 Kings 1–11 tell the story of this time, during which a kingdom was established under kings David and Solomon. What other books were written then?

6. Central to the story told in the Bible is the way God formed a family for Himself by establishing a series of covenants with various individuals. These are marked by round white icons at the top of the chart in a section called "God's Family Plan." You will learn more about these later, but for now: look carefully at each icon and notice the type of family group named in each ("One Holy Couple," for example). What do you notice about them, moving from left to right across the chart?

7. Key people and events in Bible history are arranged in chronological order across the timeline. This setion is divided into three horizontal bands representing different parts of the Middle East. The central gray area represents the land of Canaan, where most of the events take place. When the action moves out of Canaan—to the northern countries like Babylon, for example, or to the south and Egypt – they appear above or below the gray area. Look at your chart: what examples of geographic movement can you find?

8. Don't miss the events in secular history that are ranged across the bottom of the chart. Take time now to find one you are familiar with. What was going on in the development of God's plan at the same time?

STEP 4 – Closing (five minutes)

Explain that there is an optional Home Study section to reinforce each lesson and help people prepare for the next session. It is very simple to do and will not take much time (depending on how much reading they decide to do ahead). This first week, there are two parts: Understanding the Bible Timeline Chart will begin getting people familiar with the chart and how to navigate it; Looking Ahead zooms in on the first period, Early World, which is the subject of Lesson 2.

Answers to home study quetsions are printed in lighter type on the student pages of this Leader's Guide.

Recommend that participants sign up for "Your Study World" by registering as a student/participant in the Student Portal of www.BibleStudyforCatholics.com (leaders and facilitators should register through the Leader's Portal). If they enter their start date and other information asked about your group, then every week they can go to "Your Study World" for tips and encouragement related to that week's lesson.

HOME STUDY: UNDERSTANDING THE BIBLE TIMELINE CHART

- Take a few moments to familiarize yourself with the parts of the chart by reading the Key to Understanding the Bible Timeline Chart on the inside back cover of your chart..

- Review the twelve historic periods by filling in their names and color meanings in the chart below.

Period Name	Color	Color Meaning
1. Early World	turquoise	Color of the Earth from space
2. Patriarchs	burgundy	Blood of the covenant
3. Egypt & Exodus	red	Crossing of the Red Sea
4. Desert Wanderings	tan	Color of sand/the desert
5. Conquest & Judges	green	Lush hills of Canaan
6. Royal Kingdom	purple	Royal throne
7. Divided Kingdom	black	Darkness of the Divided Kingdom
8. Exile	baby blue	"Singing the blues" in "Baby-lon"
9. Return	yellow	Brighter days
10. Maccabean Revolt	orange	Oil lamps of purified Temple
11. Messianic Fulfillment	gold	Gifts of the Magi
12. The Church	white	Spotless bride of Christ

- Find the Table of Contents in your Bible. Using your chart or bookmark as a reference, highlight the fourteen narrative books. If you are not used to finding books in your Bible, take the time to locate each narrative book before you continue.

Throughout this study, Looking Ahead is a set of Home Study questions that follows the same format as the Home Study for subsequent sessions. First, a brief synopsis of the next period is given and questions are asked about it whose answers can be gleaned from the Bible Timeline chart. Then, several reading selections are offered to offer an idea of what will happen in that period. Obviously, the more selections that are read, the easier it will be to follow the stories in the next lecture. Though some participants may not have time to read ahead, encourage them to do their best.

Since answers to the Home Study questions can be gleaned directly from the chart, you do not need to go over them in class unless you think this is necessary. For your reference, they have been written directly into the student pages in the Leader's Guide.

Note: If people have trouble finding out what the color meaning is, a key to colors is printed on the last panel of the chart and the meanings are also given on the bookmark.

Prayer
Lead participants in the Responsive Prayer found on page 46 of the Student Workbook or pray the portion that applies to this lesson.

HOME STUDY: LOOKING AHEAD

*Every story has a beginning, a middle, and an end. The story of salvation history begins at the beginning of time. In the **Early World** period you will learn how the world began, what went terribly wrong, and how God promised to provide a solution.*

- Use your chart to fill in the following information:

    Period name: <u>Early World</u>   Time period: <u>Creation - 2000 BC</u>

    Period color: <u>Turquoise</u>   Color meaning: <u>The color of the Earth seen from space</u>

    Key people (list four from Jesus' bloodline):

    Adam, Seth, Noah, Shem

    Key events (five):

    Creation, the Fall, Curse & Promise, the Flood, people scattered at Babel

    Concurrent event in secular history (name one): <u>Great pyramids built, c. 2685 BC</u>

- The story of the Early World is found in Genesis 1–11. You probably know these stories already, although you may not know how they are connected. That will be explained in the next session. In the meantime, read one or more of them ahead of time, in preparation.

    Early World:

    Genesis 1–3   Creation, Adam and Eve / the Fall

    Genesis 4   Cain and Abel

    Genesis 6, 9   Noah and the Flood

    Genesis 11:1–9 The Tower of Babel

PREPARING TO LEAD SESSION 2: EARLY WORLD

- *For this session only, read all instructions to leaders, preview the DVD, and familiarize yourself with all questions and responses.*

- *Carefully read the following Lesson Overview:*

Lesson Overview

With Session 2, Jeff Cavins begins to tell the story from the beginning by giving an overview of the Early World, the earliest period on the Bible Timeline. This is one of the most important lessons of the series, for it is this part of the story that sets the plot for the rest. Readers must be able to suspend any previous notions that Adam and Eve and Noah are simply nursery stories. A proper understanding of things that happened at the dawn of time is needed if God's plan is to be understood at all.

Jeff gives guidelines for understanding this time of "pre-history," which includes the creation of the universe and the special creation of man and woman in God's image; what happened at the Fall; and early seeds of promised redemption. He goes on to tell what happens as the world is inhabited and grows wicked; how God deals with the problem by sending a flood; and how a new start is made by Noah's family. The enduring effects of original sin are seen as two sorts of civilizations arise: those who call on the name of the Lord and those who strive to make a name for themselves. The latter are exemplified in the closing scene, the Tower of Babel, as a result of which mankind ends up scattered in confusion.

LEADING THE CLASS SESSION

STEP 1: Opening Review (fifteen minutes)

- *Make certain everyone in the class has their materials and is familiar with them, particularly with the workings of the Bible Timeline chart. This will become a valuable reference tool.*

- *Explain that participants will be memorizing the periods with the help of the color-coding system they reviewed in the discussion groups last session. Notice that the first period, Early World, is colored turquoise on the chart. This color can be remembered as the color of the Earth, seen from space. Have participants find it on their memory bead wristbands. As time goes on, you will use these wristbands to jog memories as you recite the periods.*

- *Read aloud or summarize the above Lesson Overview.*

STEP 2: View DVD (thirty minutes)

The Student Workbook section for each lesson begins with a brief outline of Jeff Cavins' recorded talk for that lesson. Space is included in that outline for taking notes. Ask group members to write down at least one thing that stands out to them from the talk to share later with the class.

Covenant

NOTES

1. The Creation of the World

   Form → Time
       to chaos   Covenant → Family

   ① ② ③
   Intellect / Will → act on it   Image + likeness of God [Love]
            capacity
            to love

2. The Creation of Adam and Eve

       Covenant - Marriage   leave/cleave/become God - Don't eat / you will die

   Pride - Disordered   Nahash - Leviathan - Sea monster
       self trust
           Concupiscence   Serpent - you will not die

3. The Fall: Effects of Original Sin

   Gen 2   till/Shamar protect   Can you really trust God

                           Pride

       loss of Grace - life of soul is gone

                       Concupiscence ~

       Intellect darkened - will weakened   Ch 3:13: Proto Evangelium

4. The Promise

   3:15 -   Out of suffering - fruitful suffering =
                               Joy

   For Self
   a For God

5. Adam's Family Grows   Toledoth - the Generations of...

       Ch 5 Gen   Shem - Here
             Cain & Able ...

STEP 3: *Small group discussion (forty minutes)*

These questions for group discussion relate to the lecture for Session 2. Suggested responses are given below to help facilitators guide the discussion.

1. The main characters are Adam and Eve; Cain, Abel, and Seth; Noah; Shem, Ham, and Japheth. The main events are Creation, the Fall, curse and promise, the Flood, and the people scattered at Babel.

   To encourage discussion, ask "What did you learn from the Creation story?"

2. The choice put before Adam and Eve was literally between obeying God—by refraining from eating the fruit of the tree of the knowledge of good and evil—and following the Serpent's advise—by eating that same fruit and "becom[ing] like God, knowing good and evil" (Genesis 3:5). In essence, they were asked to choose between accepting God's rule over them and becoming their own gods. The same choice is before us today.

3. When they failed to trust God and followed the Serpent instead, Adam and Eve made a decision to go their own way instead of God's way. This had the logical consequence of removing them from God's friendship. It brought sin and corruption and pain and toil and death into the world.

4. The consequences of the Fall are evident immediately in the story. Cain kills Abel. From Cain grows a civilization that is violent and vengeful. By the time of Noah, the world is full of wickedness. Immediately after the flood, Noah gets drunk, his sons sin, and his grandson is cursed. The earth is again filled with people who seek to make a name for themselves. The people who build the Tower of Babel exemplify the choice Adam and Eve made in the garden: they have chosen not to follow God, but are going their own way instead.

5. In Genesis 3:15, God announces that the "seed of the woman" will crush the head of the "seed of the serpent"—in other words, there will one day be a battle in which a human will deal the devil a death blow.

   The fact that God barred further access to the tree of life actually offers a second ray of hope to the situation: His children will not be allowed to make their separated state permanent.

6. The consequences of the Fall are so ingrained that not even wiping out the "bad guys" and starting over with a righteous man (Noah) makes a difference. The post-flood population is no better than the people who preceded it. The effects of the Fall will not be limited to those who caused it. What we are seeing is "original sin": internal consequences passed on through the generations. Something more will need to be done.

DISCUSSION QUESTIONS

1. The story of the Early World is told in Genesis chapters 1–11. Locate the Early World period on your *Bible Timeline* chart. Who are the main characters, and what are the main events?

2. What choice were Adam and Eve given in the Garden of Eden?

3. What were the consequences of that choice, both for them and for us?

4. How can you see those consequences in the lives of the people that follow?

5. Turn to Genesis 3:15 in your Bible. What hope is given at the outset of the story that the situation will be redeemed?

6. In the story of Noah, we see God deal with the mounting wickedness by destroying the earth with a flood. Did that solution to the problem work? Why or why not?

7. The people of Babel's desire to "make a name for themselves" sets them against those, like Noah, who call on God's name. As a consequence, God confuses their languages and scatters them across the earth. Their inability to communicate and their scattered state are in effect a vivid physical manifestation of their spiritual reality.

8. If people have trouble answering this question, prompt them by asking it in other ways: Have you ever had to choose between doing what you want and doing what you know God wants you to do? Are you ever tempted to define good and evil for yourself, instead of listening to what God says is right or wrong? Etc.

STEP 4: Closing

Gather discussion groups together for the close. Have each share one thing they learned or ask them together to comment on the significance of the period. Before closing, explain the Home Study assignment for the following session, which will be period 2: Patriarchs.

Prayer:

Introduce participants to the Responsive Prayer found on page 46 of the Student Workbook. If there is time, pray through the entire prayer using the memory beads as you read. In subsequent lessons, you may do the same or pray just the portion that applies to that lesson (see Closing Prayer on opposite page).

Handling Questions

Decide ahead of time how you will handle questions about the Bible that come up in the course of this study. Determine if there is someone knowledgeable in the group who can answer them, either during or after class, or whether you will refer participants to good Catholic resources (see some suggestions below).

Keep in mind that the purpose of this course is to give people a "quick journey" through the Bible to help them get their bearings by providing an outline of the Story and helping them remember it. They will have the rest of their lives to build on this general understanding. As a leader, you may need to make a particular effort to keep the group focused on the "big picture." It will be worth it in the long run, for knowing that big picture gives a solid foundation for continuing to learn.

If someone in your group is continually distracted by details, remind them of these things and suggest that they write questions inside the back cover of their workbook or on a separate sheet of paper so that they can go back to them later. Consider offering The Bible Timeline: The Story of Salvation as a follow-up course for those who want to go deeper.

Here are a few resources you may want to recommend: Catechism of the Catholic Church, Catholic Bible Dictionary (New York: Doubleday, 2009), You Can Understand the Bible by Peter Kreeft (San Francisco: Ignatius Press, 2005), Catholic Encyclopedia (available at www.newadvent.org).

7. Describe the condition of mankind at the close of the Early World period.

8. Do you ever face choices today that are in any way like the choice put before Adam and Eve? Explain.

CLOSING PRAYER

God's plan unfolded through history and gives us the Story for our lives. Let us pray in the name of Jesus:

In the early World, you created the heavens and Earth and tested Adam and Eve in the garden:

–Help us to always choose the life that you offer.

Our Father…

HOME STUDY: LOOKING AHEAD

By the end of the Early World period, Adam and Eve's descendents have spread throughout the known world. For the rest of the book of Genesis (which narrates the period of the Patriarchs) the story focuses on one man, Abraham, with whom God will establish an everlasting promise of blessing. His descendants will be God's chosen people, Israel, and through them God will bless the entire world.

- Use your chart to fill in the following information about this time period:

   Period name: <u>Patriarchs</u>   Time period: <u>2000 BC - 1700 BC</u>

   Period color: <u>Burgundy</u>   Color meaning: <u>God's blood covenant with Abraham</u>

   Key people (list at least four): Abraham, Isaac, Jacob, Judah or Joseph (also Sarah, Ishmael, Melchizedek, Perez, or any of Jacob's sons)

   What appears to be the most important event? <u>Abrahamic Covenant</u>

   What nation is the current world power? <u>Egypt</u>

- The story of the Patriarchs period is full of action and many memorable stories, some of them central not just to Israel's history but to Christian history as well. If reading Genesis 12–50 is too much, try reading one or more of the following vignettes.

   Patriarchs:

Genesis 12:1–9	God calls Abraham
Genesis 15, 17, 22	God's covenant with Abraham
Genesis 25:19–34	Jacob and Esau
Genesis 29:1–30:24	Jacob gets married; Jacob's children
Genesis 32:22–32	Jacob wrestles with God and gets a new name
Genesis 37–50	Joseph and his brothers: to get just the gist of the story, focus on chapters 37 and 41–44

PREPARING TO LEAD SESSION 3: PATRIARCHS

- For this session only, read all instructions to leaders, preview the DVD, and familiarize yourself with all questions and responses.

- Carefully read the following Lesson Overview:

The sin itself contains the ofence seal of the punishment.

Lesson Overview

Session 3, Patriarchs, covers the rest of Genesis and the stories of Abraham, Isaac, Jacob, and Joseph: the forefathers of Israel. Jeff Cavins zooms in on the central feature of this period in light of the "big picture" of God's plan, which is the everlasting covenant God establishes with Abraham. This three-fold promise of land, kingdom, and worldwide blessing forms a framework for the events of the rest of the Bible, which shows how God delivers on these three promises.

Other key events covered in the teaching tape are God's call of Abraham; the climactic point at which God asks Abraham to trust Him by offering up his beloved son Isaac; and the passing down of God's promise and blessing through Isaac, Jacob, and Jacob's sons. Joseph is presented as a figure of Christ, as one who reconciles his brethren to their father.

LEADING THE CLASS SESSION

STEP 1: Opening Review (fifteen minutes)
- Review the way the Early World set the stage for the rest of the story by reading aloud last week's Lesson Overview (p. L-7) or by asking participants what they remember.

- We now move on to Period 2, Patriarchs—which is burgundy on the chart, representing the blood covenant God will make with Abraham. Read or explain in your own words the Lesson Overview (above).

- Use the memory bead wristbands to review the two colors/periods to date.

- Using the map in the Student Workbook on page 13, describe the Fertile Crescent and point out the main cities and areas on which the story will be played: Ur, Haran, and the land of Canaan/Promised Land.

STEP 2: View DVD (thirty minutes)
The Student Workbook section for each lesson begins with a brief outline of Jeff Cavins' talk. Space is included for taking notes. Ask group members to write down at least one thing that stands out to them from the talk to share later with the class.

NOTES

1. God calls Abraham

    — Righteous Men
    Do I trust God

2. God makes a covenant with Abraham

    • Land Promise (Genesis 15)

    • Kingdom Promise (Genesis 17)
    ("I will make your name great" = royal dynasty)

    • Promise of Worldwide Blessing (Genesis 22)

3. God asks Abraham to trust Him

    God will provide the lamb
    Ram sacrificed
    continues to look in scrip for lamb

4. The promise and blessing passed down

    • Isaac

    • Jacob

    • Jacob's sons

This chart shows that God's three promises to Abraham are strengthened in new covenants made with Moses and David and come to fulfillment in the New Covenant of Jesus Christ. It also shows how God's family grows from One Holy Couple with Adam and Eve and One Holy Family under Noah and so on, until it becomes One Holy Catholic and Apostolic Church—all through the means of God's covenant promises. Students can refer back to this chart if they need to later on.

When you get to the questions on page 14 (or during the closing), you might want to refer this "Covenantal Structure of Salvation History" chart. It will help participants remember the way Jeff Cavins explained the development over time of God's covenant with Abraham.

The bottom portion of the page, which shows the growth of God's family by covenant, will be addressed in Session 4.

THE COVENANTAL STRUCTURE OF SALVATION HISTORY

The charts below diagram the way salvation history can be viewed as unfolding through a series of covenants God made with his people. Adam and Eve were created in a close relationship with God that was shattered at the Fall, a relationship that is later most closely imaged by families and by bonds of kinship that are created through covenantal promises. God moved to restore humanity to relationship with himself by means of a series of covenants.

The first diagram shows how God later expands on aspects of the initial promise he made to Abraham in Genesis 12. Each of these covenantal promises to Abraham and his descendants (of land, kingdom, and worldwide blessing) is fulfilled in a future covenant: the Mosaic Covenant, the Davidic Covenant, and the New Covenant in Jesus Christ:

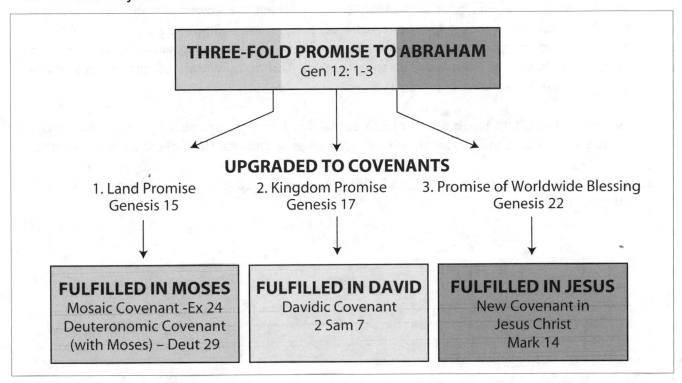

This diagram shows the progressive growth of God's family from One Holy Couple to One Holy Catholic and Apostolic Church, illustrated by means of these same covenants:

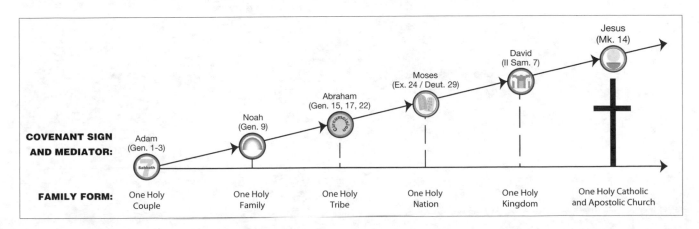

1. God's first step toward restoring his scattered people to Himself was not to reach out to gather everyone back in. Rather, He began by calling one man, Abram, to leave everything behind (to leave, in fact, that area of the world in which the Tower of Babel was built and which is even today known for the remains of its ziggurats or imposing stepped-towers)— to leave everything behind and follow Him to a new land which He would show him. The restoration is implicit within the blessing he gives Abram, by whom "all the families of the earth will bless themselves" (verse 3).

2. Abraham, Isaac, and Jacob are the main patriarchs. Some people also include as patriarchs Jacob's sons—particularly Joseph, whose story takes up the final third of the book of Genesis.

3. Burgundy is the color of blood, and blood is what sealed the covenant God made with Abraham.

DISCUSSION QUESTIONS

1. We last saw mankind scattered, their languages confused, after trying to build a name for themselves rather than calling on the name of the Lord. What was God's first step toward restoring them to Himself? (See Genesis 12:1)

2. *Patriarchs* means literally "fathers" in the sense that we use it in "forefathers" or "founding fathers." This period tells of the patriarchs—the founding fathers—of the nation of Israel. Who are they?

3. Why is the color burgundy used to represent this time period?

Abraham's Journey

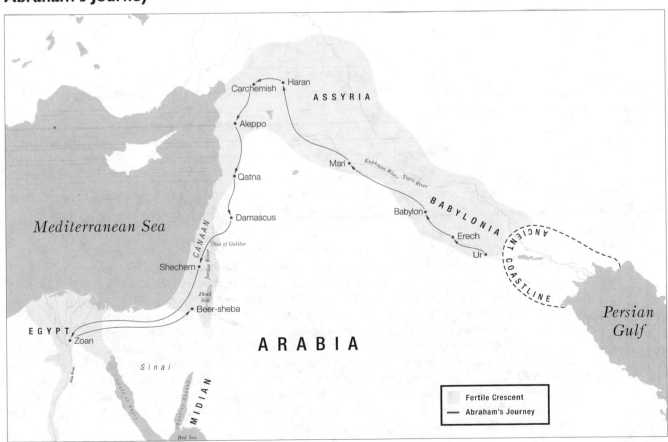

4. Genesis 12:1-3 says: "Now the LORD said to Abram, 'Go from your country and your kindred and your father's house to the land that I will show you. And I will make of you a great nation, and I will bless you, and make your name great, so that you will be a blessing. I will bless those who bless you, and him who curses you I will curse; and by you all the families of the earth shall bless themselves.'"

This promise can be broken into three parts: a promise of land for his many descendants; a promise of nation and a great name; and a promise of worldwide blessing. The chart lists the second promise as a promise of royal kingdom because later on in Genesis, God tells Abraham that this is His plan for them.

Notice that in the fulfillment of this promise, and in return for Abraham's faithful obedience, God will give Abraham's family what he did not allow the people at Babel to achieve for themselves.

Note: As the weeks go on, if you find that looking up these passages takes up too much time, you might assign them ahead of time or come with a Bible already marked that you can pass to the person who will do the reading.

5. The promises of God passed down from Abraham to his son (by Sarah) Isaac; to his son Jacob; and from Jacob to his sons Judah and Joseph (through his sons Ephraim and Manasseh). Eventually, the promise would extend to all mankind.

Read the paragraphs following question 5 aloud to make sure everyone understands the concept of covenant and the promises God makes to Abraham.

6. Answers will vary based on familiarity with the story. It is not for nothing that Abraham is known as the father of all who have faith. Here is a litany of examples from Hebrews 11:8-19:

> By faith Abraham obeyed when he was called to go out to a place which he was to receive as an inheritance; and he went out, not knowing where he was to go. By faith he sojourned in the land of promise, as in a foreign land, living in tents with Isaac and Jacob, heirs with him of the same promise. For he looked forward to the city which has foundations, whose builder and maker is God. By faith Sarah herself received power to conceive, even when she was past the age, since she considered him faithful who had promised. Therefore from one man, and him as good as dead, were born descendants as many as the stars of heaven and as the innumerable grains of sand by the seashore…. By faith Abraham, when he was tested, offered up Isaac, and he who had received the promises was ready to offer up his only son, of whom it was said, "Through Isaac shall your descendants be named." He considered that God was able to raise men even from the dead; hence, figuratively speaking, he did receive him back.

4. Find and read Genesis 12:1–3. What promises did God make to Abraham?

5. To whom did the promises pass in the following generations?

Those promises to Abraham are elaborated on later in his life, in Genesis 15, 17, and 22. Each time the promise builds until it becomes a *covenant* promise to give Abraham's descendants a land, to establish them as a kingdom, and to make them a source of worldwide blessing.

What is a covenant?

A covenant is a binding oath that forms an unbreakable family bond between two parties. God's help is invoked to help maintain the bond. It is established by means of a solemn oath sealed with blood. There are blessings promised to those who keep the covenant, and curses to those who break it.

This *Abrahamic covenant* gives us a blueprint for understanding the rest of the Bible, which is basically the story of the way God makes good on those promises. Look at the Patriarchs period of your chart to get an idea of where the story is going in the future. Each time God fulfills one of the promises, He will make another covenant with His people. From the "Abrahamic Covenant" box, identify the people through whom future covenants will be made, that bring to fulfillment the three promises made to Abraham:

Land promise: _____Moses_____

Kingdom promise: _____David_____

Promise of worldwide blessing: _____Jesus Christ_____

6. Over and over, the question is posed to mankind: will you trust God? In what ways did Abraham demonstrate his obedient trust over the course of his lifetime?

7. Answers will vary. Encourage continued discussion by adding a question or two such as: What makes it hard or easy to follow in that area? Does anything you learned from this lesson inspire you or give you strength?

STEP 4: Closing
Gather discussion groups together for the close. Have each share one thing they learned or ask them together to comment on the significance of the period.

Our pace increases after this week and from now on we will take two periods at a time. The next session will cover periods 3 and 4, Egypt and Exodus and Desert Wanderings. Remind participants that the home study assignment will have them glean important aspects of those periods from the chart before recommending some reading selections from Exodus and Numbers.

Prayer:
Lead participants in the Responsive Prayer found on page 46 of the Student Workbook or just pray the portion that applies to this lesson (see Closing Prayer on opposite page).

7. How might God be calling you to trust in Him today?

CLOSING PRAYER:

God's plan unfolded through history and gives us the Story for our lives. Let us pray in the name of Jesus:

In the time of the Patriarchs, you called Abraham and promised his children land, a royal kingdom, and worldwide blessing:

–Help us always to hope in your promises.

Our Father...

HOME STUDY: LOOKING AHEAD

The next session will cover two time periods. Notice on your chart that the first, Egypt and Exodus, spans about 400 years. Little is known about much of this time. When our story opens, Jacob's family (also called "Israel") has been in Egypt for generations. When a new Pharaoh comes to power and enslaves them, they cry out to God for deliverance. God takes them out of Egypt, punishing the Egyptians and demonstrating His power through the dramatic events of the Passover. He then establishes them as His own people, "a kingdom of priests and a holy nation."

In spite of the many miracles God works in order to free Israel from slavery, His people refuse to fully trust Him. The following forty-year period of Desert Wanderings is both a punishment and an opportunity to learn to trust God and prepare to conquer and live in the land of Canaan.

- Use your chart to fill in the following information about these time periods:

Period name: <u>Egypt and Exodus</u>   Time period: _____1700 BC - 1280 BC_____

Period color: _____Red_____   Color meaning: _____The Red Sea_____

Key person (Whom does God send?): _____Moses_____

Current event in secular history: _____Building projects of Pharoahs Seti I & Ramses II_____

Period name: <u>Desert Wanderings</u>   Time period: _____1280 BC - 1240 BC_____

Period color: _____Tan_____   Color meaning: _____Color of the desert sands_____

Key events (list two): _____Covenant in Moab_____

_____12 spies sent out_____

Supplemental book for this period: _____Deuteronomy_____

- In the future you may want to read all of Exodus and Numbers. For now, choose one or more of the following passages to read before the next class, to give you a feel for these time periods.

Egypt and Exodus:

Exodus 3	Moses and the burning bush
Exodus 7–10	Plagues on Egypt
Exodus 11–14	The last plague (Passover), the Exodus, the Red Sea
Exodus 32	The golden calf

Desert Wanderings:

Numbers 13–14	Rebellion and forty years of wandering
Numbers 25	Israel's apostasy with the Baal of Peor

PREPARING TO LEAD SESSION 4: EGYPT & EXODUS, DESERT WANDERINGS

- *For this session only, read all instructions to leaders, preview the DVD, and familiarize yourself with all questions and responses.*

- *Carefully read the following Lesson Overview:*

Lesson Overview

Session 4 covers periods 3 and 4 on The Bible Timeline chart: Egypt and Exodus and Desert Wanderings. At the close of the Patriarchs, Jacob's family moved down South to Egypt to escape famine. In the intervening years they have been made slaves of a new Pharaoh and are crying out to God. Jeff Cavins tells the exciting story of how God liberates His people from bondage through the agency of His servant Moses. Jeff also explains how the plagues are actually attacks made on the false gods of the Egyptians and how God's signs and wonders reveal His sovereign power.

Following their release from Egypt, God gives Israel the Law and directions to build a Tabernacle, a place where His presence will rest among them. The children of Israel enter a kind of "boot camp" in the desert, in which God teaches them to trust Him. Their failure leads to forty years of wandering in the desert while a new generation learns to walk in faith.

LEADING THE CLASS SESSION

STEP 1: Opening Review (fifteen minutes)
- *Begin with a brief review of the story thus far, using the Lesson Overviews on pages L-7 and L-11. Due to the importance to the overall story of both the Early World and Patriarchs periods, it will be worthwhile to cover highlights of both. Use the memory bead wristband to review the progression of periods so far and to introduce the next two periods: Egypt and Exodus, which can be remembered by the red of the Red Sea, and Desert Wanderings, which is represented by the tan of the desert sands.*

- *Introduce the new lesson by reading or giving in your own words the Lesson Overview above. Those who did the Home Study for this session will be familiar with the way these periods are represented on the Bible Timeline chart. Take this opportunity to illustrate the way geographic movement is shown between the "Northern Countries" at the top (out of which Abram was called during the time of the Patriarchs), the Land of Canaan in the middle, and "South and Egypt" at the bottom. A large arrow indicates the movement of Jacob and his family down to Egypt prior to the start of Egypt and Exodus, and the angling of the red bloodline shows them moving out of Egypt and back to Canaan through the Desert Wanderings.*

- *If you have time, point out the icons that appear to the right of "God's Family Plan" at the top of the chart, starting in the Early World period and moving to the right. Ask someone to point out the first three and explain how God's family has grown so far, and then notice the new one (One Holy Nation under the covenant mediator Moses) that will be explained during this session. This progression is also illustrated at the bottom of the Covenantal Structure of Salvation History chart on page 12.*

STEP 2: View DVD (thirty minutes)
The Student Workbook section for each lesson begins with a brief outline of Jeff Cavins' talk. Space is included for taking notes. Ask group members to write down at least one thing that stands out to them from the talk to share later with the class.

Egypt & Exodus
Desert Wanderings

God Leads Israel out of Bondage
Israel Must Learn to Trust God

NOTES

1. God delivers Israel from slavery in Egypt

2. God makes a covenant with Israel

3. Israel fails to trust God

4. Forty years in the desert

[Handwritten margin notes:]

Exodus + Numbers
Red/Fam

① hit the midpoint

② last 3 sessions we went through the creation story, Noah and the re-establishment of our relationship w God after the fall

— We covered the 3fold promise of land, nation and blessing to Abraham
Moses
David
Jesus
Joseph the dreamer and his family reunion w

open bibles to exodus take at least one note per section of outline to share.

Students may want to refer to this map and diagram later,
when they return to Exodus to read it for themselves.

The Ten Commandments can be found in Exodus 20 and Deuteronomy 5.

Proposed Route of the Exodus and Wanderings in the Desert

(The exact route across the Red Sea is not known for certain)

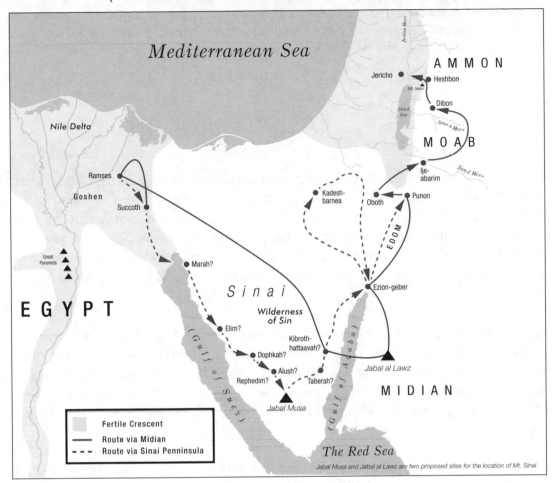

Mediterranean Sea

AMMON

Jericho • — Heshbon
Mt. Nebo ▲
Dibon

Dead Sea

Arno'n River

MOAB

Zared River

Ije-abarim

Nile Delta

Ramses •
Goshen
Succoth •

Kadesh-barnea •   Oboth •   Punon •

EDOM

Great Pyramids ▲▲▲

Marah? •

Sinai

Wilderness of Sin

EGYPT

Ezion-geber •

(Gulf of Suez)

Elim? •

Kibroth-hattaavah? •

Dophkah? •

Alush? •   Taberah? •

Rephidim? •

Jabal al Lawz ▲

(Gulf of Aqaba)

MIDIAN

Jabal Musa ▲

Jordan River

Legend:
- Fertile Crescent
- —— Route via Midian
- - - - Route via Sinai Penninsula

The Red Sea

Jabal Musa and Jabal al Lawz are two proposed sites for the location of Mt. Sinai

Plan of the Tabernacle *(Exodus 40:16-34)* and
Arrangements of Tribal Camps *(Numbers 2)*

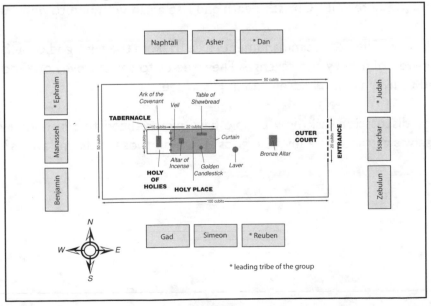

| Naphtali | Asher | * Dan |

* Ephraim

* Judah

Manasseh

Issachar

Benjamin

Zebulun

TABERNACLE

Ark of the Covenant
Veil
Table of Shewbread

50 cubits

10 cubits   20 cubits

Curtain

OUTER COURT

ENTRANCE

20 cubits

HOLY OF HOLIES

Altar of Incense
Golden Candlestick
Laver

Bronze Altar

HOLY PLACE

100 cubits

| Gad | Simeon | * Reuben |

N
W — E
S

* leading tribe of the group

STEP 3: Small group discussion (forty minutes)
These questions for group discussion pertain to the taped lecture for Session 4. Suggested responses are given below to help facilitators guide the discussion. Get the discussion started by asking: "What stood out to you in the DVD and why?" Ask students to share something memorable they wrote down while listening to Jeff Cavins' talk.

1. Israel has not heard from God for 400 years and they are slaves in a foreign land. What about the promises God made to Abraham, Isaac, and Jacob to give them the land of Canaan? Where was God? Did He know of their plight? These words told Moses that the same God who spoke to Abraham and made those great promises; the same God who gave Abraham and Sarah Isaac in their old age; the same God who watched over Jacob for all those years and reaffirmed His promises was alive and well and listening and ready to make good on His Word.

2. Again and again, God says He will do a thing so that Israel and Egypt will know that He is the Lord. The original word that is here translated "Lord" is YHWH—"I AM," the name God revealed to Moses at the burning bush, the God who made the promises to Abraham, Isaac, and Jacob. In the plagues, He reveals even more about Himself: to begin with, that He is greater and more powerful than any of the gods of Egypt, which He slays one by one with impunity.

3. God struck the first born sons of Egypt in the final plague, in which the angel of death passed over the land of Egypt and slew all but those covered by the sign of blood on the doorway. The annual Jewish remembrance of this event is the Passover.

4. The crossing of the Red Sea prefigures baptism, in which we are freed by water from sin. In this sacrament we enter into Christ's death and rise again with him to new life.

5. Answers will vary. The Ten Commandments free us from the false god of self; from the gods of lust and power, of money and revenge. They free us to set our eyes on God and live as we were created to live, as His children and in His image.

To encourage discusssion, ask how people have experienced this in their lives. Have they found themselves attracted to any false gods? How do those gods enslave us?

DISCUSSION QUESTIONS

1. God introduced Himself to Moses as "the God of Abraham, the God of Isaac, and the God of Jacob" (from the burning bush, Exodus 3:6). What did that tell Moses about God?

2. What important message did the ten plagues send to Egypt and Israel?

3. God told Pharaoh, if you will not free my firstborn son, then I will kill your firstborn son. How did He accomplish this, and what is the name of the annual remembrance of this event?

4. Think about it: In the Red Sea crossing, the children of Israel were freed from their enemy by passing through water. What New Covenant sacrament does this prefigure? Explain.

5. The first terms of the Sinai Covenant are what we know as the Ten Commandments, which John Paul II called "the law of freedom: not the freedom to follow our blind passions, but the freedom to love, to choose what is good in every situation, even when to do so is a burden" (*Celebration of the Word at Mount Sinai,* St. Catherine's Monastery, 26 February 2000). Think about the Ten Commandments. What kinds of "false gods" do they free us from?

6. The Tabernacle signified the presence of God dwelling among His people. This is the first time we have seen this since God walked with Adam and Eve in the Garden of Eden. It is a sign of and a step toward restoration of the broken relationship.

7. The Levites, who alone rallied to Moses and the Lord when Moses confronted the people with their sin, were set apart to the Lord as priests.

8. When Moses sent twelve spies into the land of Canaan, they brought back a report that it was fertile and full of giants. Ten spies felt the foes were too mighty to defeat; only two stressed the bounty of the land and said that God would lead them in. Because the people listened to the ten and did not trust God to take them safely into the land and give it to them (in spite of the way He had delivered them from Egypt), He made them wander a year in the desert for every day the spies had been in the land. This would allow a generation to grow up learning to trust entirely on God's providence.

   If time allows, ask whether anyone has experienced wandering in their lives. What did they learn?

9. Answers will vary; encourage discussion. You might also ask why it will be important for the Israelites to teach their children. What might happen if they do not? Is this important for us today? Why or why not?

STEP 4: Closing
Gather discussion groups together for the close. Have each share one thing they learned or ask them together to comment on the significance of the period.

Explain the home study assignment for the following week, which will be periods 5 and 6, Conquest and Judges and Royal Kingdom.

Prayer:
Lead participants in the Responsive Prayer found on page 46 of the Student Workbook or just pray the portion that applies to this lesson (see Closing Prayer on opposite page).

6. What did the Tabernacle signify to Israel?

7. Which tribe was given the priesthood after Israel's unfaithfulness with the golden calf?

8. Why did God make Israel wander for forty years in the desert, and what was He trying to teach them?

9. St. Paul tells us that these stories "were written down for our instruction" (1 Corinthians 10:11). What message do they carry for you today?

CLOSING PRAYER

God's plan unfolded through history and gives us the Story for our lives. Let us pray in the name of Jesus:

You freed your people from slavery so they could worship you:

—Free us from sin so we can serve and worship as we ought.

You taught Israel to trust you through forty years of wanderings:

—Help us to trust in you, O God.

Our Father...

HOME STUDY: LOOKING AHEAD

The next session will cover two periods: Conquest and Judges and Royal Kingdom. After forty years in the desert, Israel enters Canaan, the Promised Land. God's first promise to Abraham is fulfilled. However, Israel's failure to keep God's commandments leads to sin, oppression, and an incomplete possession of the land.

The people of Israel grow weary of being led by judges and so they demand a king "like all the nations" (1 Sam 8:5). God's second promise to Abraham—that of an everlasting royal kingdom—is fulfilled in King David.

- Use your chart to fill in the following information about these time periods:

    Period name: <u>Conquest and Judges</u>   Time period: ___1240 BC - 1050 BC___

    Period color: ___Green___   Color meaning: ___The green hills of Canaan___

    Narrative Books: ___Joshua, Judges, the beginning of 1 Samuel___

    List any names familiar to you and tell what you know of them: _____
    Answers will vary. Some of the familiar names are Deborah, Gideon, and Samson among
    the Judges; Samuel and Jesse, Rahab and Ruth.

    Period name: <u>Royal Kingdom</u>   Time period: ___1050 BC - 930 BC___

    Period color: ___Purple___   Color meaning: ___Royalty___

    Key people: ___Saul, David, Solomon___

    What would you say is the key event? ___God's Covenant with David___

- So many wonderful stories take place during the periods of Conquest and Judges and Royal Kingdom, it is difficult to narrow down the reading. Choose some or all of the following to get an overview of the periods, but make sure to return in the future to this important stage in God's Plan.

Conquest and Judges:

Joshua 2	Rahab and the spies
Joshua 6	The Fall of Jericho
Judges 1:1–3:6	Conquest; overview of sin cycle
Judges 13–16	Samson and Delilah

These two maps properly belong to the following Session.
They are printed here so that students can refer to them when they are reading ahead.

Royal Kingdom:

1 Samuel 8	Israel asks for a king
2 Samuel 7	God makes a covenant with David
1 Kings 9; 11:1–13	Solomon's reign and folly

The Conquest of Canaan

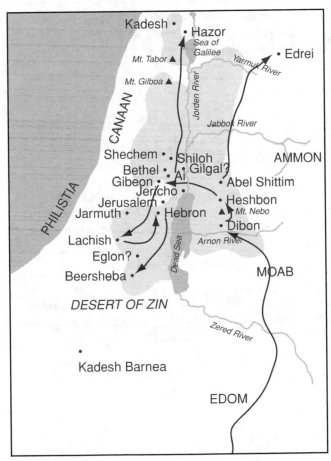

Israel–The Twelve Tribes

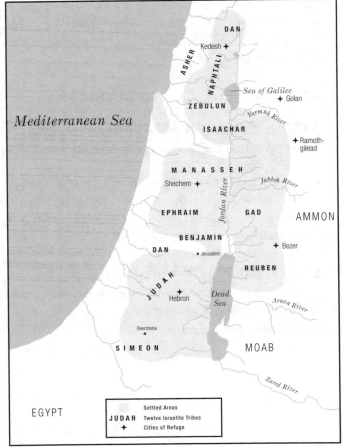

PREPARING TO LEAD SESSION 5: CONQUEST & JUDGES, ROYAL KINGDOM

- *For this session only, read all instructions to leaders, preview the DVD, and familiarize yourself with all questions and responses.*

- *Carefully read the following Lesson Overview:*

Lesson Overview

In Session 5, the children of Israel finally reach their long-time goal and enter the Promised Land. Jeff explains how Joshua leads them triumphantly in and settles the land. Ultimately, however, they do not obey God's command to conquer Canaan completely. Not only that, they fail to teach their children about God and after just one generation, crisis strikes. A cycle ensues in which Israel falls into first sin and then, because of that sin, servitude to the surrounding nations. They cry out to help (supplication) and God raises a judge to bring about their salvation. Next follows a period of silence before the cycle starts over again.

After seven cycles and a total of twelve judges, Israel has had enough and cries out for a king to rule them "like the other nations." They have rejected the rule of God, but He will eventually rule them again through His chosen one. Jeff covers the reigns of the first three kings: Saul, who unites the kingdom; David, who expands it; and Solomon, who builds it. The period ends, sadly, with the sins of Solomon and the looming division of the once-glorious kingdom.

LEADING THE CLASS SESSION

STEP 1: Opening Review (fifteen minutes)

- *Begin with a brief review of the previous lesson, using the Lesson Overview on page L-17.*

- *Introduce the two new periods, Conquest and Judges and Royal Kingdom, reading or giving in your own words this week's Lesson Overview (above). Explain their colors: green for the green hills of Canaan and purple, the color of royalty. Review the first six periods using the memory bead wristbands. You might ask whether anyone can recite them unaided.*

STEP 2: View DVD (thirty minutes)

The Student Workbook section for each lesson begins with a brief outline of Jeff Cavins' talk. Space is included for taking notes. Ask group members to write down at least one thing that stands out to them from the talk to share later with the class.

NOTES

1. Joshua leads Israel into the Promised Land

   - Land
   - King
   - worldwide blessing

   - water rolled 8 miles back
   save cities
   holicost —
   sm of one affects us all.

   Rehab — Harlot
   in Jesus
   (Mentioned in Jesus' genealogy)

   God shows self
   unique
   powerful
   the one true God

2. Israel fails to teach her children about God

   Deborah
   Warrior Kings
   Samson
   Delila — night

   Ruth — great grandmother of David

   Rehab — Gentiles are part of family

   Ruth → my God will be your god

   Deborah
   Boaz
   Buzz
   Night
   Delilah
   Samson Sunlight

3. Israel asks for a king

   • Saul

   Chosen as king
   Saul doubts God

   • David – the Royal Kingdom established (2 Samuel 7)

   covenant – Dynasty

   Psalms – David being chased by Saul

   2 Sam 7:
   9
   14

   666 grant womam

   • Solomon

STEP 3: *Small group discussion (forty minutes)*

These questions for group discussion pertain to the taped lecture for Session 5. Suggested responses are given below to help facilitators guide the discussion. Get the discussion started by asking: "What stood out to you in the DVD and why?" Ask students to share something memorable they wrote down while listening to Jeff Cavins' talk.

1. The generation that entered the Promised Land was—with the exception of Joshua and Caleb—the children of those who had crossed the Red Sea. In the forty years of wandering, the original generation had died out. This new generation had spent their entire lives experiencing God's provision (food, water, shoes that didn't wear out; healing, protection from and victory over enemies). In the new land they would be tempted to forget God and follow pagan gods instead. But remembering God and obeying His commands would be crucial to their success and well-being. Unfortunately they did not teach their children or obey God. In a shockingly short time—just one generation—an entire generation grew up who did not know God or what He had done for Israel. They left God, did evil in His sight, and worshiped other gods. As a result they were delivered over to their enemies.

2. Under Joshua, Israel did exactly as the Lord commanded Moses and successfully conquered the bulk of the land.. At his death, all that remained was for Israel to finish pushing out the inhabitants, cleanse the land of pagan altars, and occupy her inheritance. But the new generation did not know God; they not only allowed the Canaanites to remain, they began worshiping their gods and doing evil in God's eyes.

    Note: Many have a hard time with the story of the conquest of Canaan. They wonder how a good God could command His people to destroy so many "innocents." This part of the story must be read in the context of the larger story. Previously, God showed Himself greater than the false gods of the world. Now He is reclaiming for Himself part of the territory that has been taken over, since the Fall, by the enemy. In turn, He will establish Israel as His people and they are charged to be living witnesses of His righteous rule. The necessary pre-requisite to this is a cleansing of the land. If they fail to follow God's ways, they themselves will lose their place in God's land (which in fact will happen, later in the story).

3. We have already seen how those who stand against God are prone to sin and wicked practices. Violence, polygamy, slavery, sorcery, even human sacrifice are the hallmark of the cultures Israel has been commanded to dispossess. Those who are squeamish about destroying them might read the book of Judges right to its horrifying close. It shows vividly the way Israel, which has failed to fully conquer the Canaanites, falls under the influence of her neighbors and becomes like them. It is hard to imagine anyone thinking that the depths of religious and moral corruption to which they sink to is something to be desired or protected.

    Israel's sin in forsaking God led to defeat by their enemies and servitude. In anguish they cried out to God ("supplication") and He raised up judges to deliver them ("salvation"). A period of peace and silence was soon followed once again by sin, and the cycle began again. This happens seven times during the time of the Judges.

4. Tired of the endless cycle of subjection to the other nations, Israel cries out for a king "like all the other nations."

DISCUSSION QUESTIONS

1. Before he died, Moses told Israel how to live in order to receive God's blessing in the Promised Land. Read Deuteronomy 6:4-9 out loud (it is printed below). This passage is kept alive today by Jews all over the world, who must pray the *Shema*, as it is called, each morning and night. You heard today about Israel's conquest of the land. Did they follow Moses' advice? What happened?

The *Shema* (Deuteronomy 6:4-9)

"Hear, O Israel: The LORD our God is one LORD; and you shall love the LORD your God with all your heart, and with all your soul, and with all your might. And these words which I command you this day shall be upon your heart; and you shall teach them diligently to your children, and shall talk of them when you sit in your house, and when you walk by the way, and when you lie down, and when you rise. And you shall bind them as a sign upon your hand, and they shall be as frontlets between your eyes. And you shall write them on the doorposts of your house and on your gates."

---

2. How well did Israel follow God's command to possess the land of Canaan?

3. Explain the seven-fold cycle Israel experienced during the time of the Judges.

4. At the close of the period of Conquest and Judges, what plea did Israel make?

5. King Saul was the first king of Israel. He was not to be like other kings, but subject to God and His Word. Saul's great contribution was to unite the kingdom. He does well to begin with, but ultimately fails to trust God. He is twice disobedient, sacrificing when he is not supposed to and sparing the life of an evil king God says to destroy. As a result, the kingdom is torn away and will be given to a man with a heart after God.

6. God's second promise to Abraham was one of kingdom. God reiterated that promise to David and made a covenant with him, promising to build a royal dynasty from him that would last forever. (A dynasty is a succession of kings in the same bloodline.)

7. Solomon made the mistake of taking 700 wives of royal birth and 300 concubines. These turned his heart away from God to the point that he followed other gods and even built altars to Chemosh and Molech and others so his wives could worship them.

8. People will have varying answers to this question. Encourage discussion by asking things like "What does it mean to have a heart like God's?" "How did David show these qualities?" and so on. You might ask them to consider why Saul lost the kingdom for his sins, while David sinned with Bathsheba yet received an everlasting promise. What was different about David?

STEP 4: Closing
Gather discussion groups together for the close. Have each share one thing they learned or ask them together to comment on the significance of the period.

Explain the Home Study assignment for the following week. Because we are now halfway through the timeline, this session's Home Study begins with a review of all the periods so far, their color names, and the meaning of those colors. It will then introduce periods 7 and 8, Divided Kingdom and Exile, in the usual manner.

Prayer:
Lead participants in the Responsive Prayer found on page 46 of the Student Workbook or just pray the portion that applies to this lesson (see Closing Prayer on opposite page).

5. Who was the first king of Israel, and how did he fare?

6. Read 2 Samuel 7:1-16. How did the Davidic covenant fulfill and expand upon God's second promise to Abraham?

7. King Solomon was the wisest man who ever lived. What caused him to turn away from God? (1 Kings 11:4-6).

8. God said David was "a man after His own heart" (1 Samuel 13:14). What qualities do you think that means that David had, that you might want to emulate?

CLOSING PRAYER

God's plan unfolded through history and gives us the Story for our lives. Let us pray in the name of Jesus:

You led Israel triumphantly into the Promised Land. They failed to teach their children, and instead did what was right in their own eyes:

—Help us to keep our eyes on you and bring up our children in your way.

You established a kingdom on your servant David and promised him an eternal throne:

—Establish Your kingdom in our midst.

Our Father...

*When you tell participants that this will be part of the Home Study for this lesson,
you might suggest that they can take the descriptive phrase from the Responsive Prayer
on page 46 if they have trouble describing the period on their own.*

HOME STUDY: REVIEW

We are half-way through the Bible Timeline chart. Take a moment to review the periods you have covered so far, using the memory beads to test your memory. What are the period names? What does each color stand for? What is a simple phrase you can use to remember what each period is about (use titles from each lesson or make up your own)? Fill out the chart below.

	Period Name	Color	Meaning	Phrase
1	Early World	Turquoise	The color of Earth seen from space	God created heaven and earth and tested Adam and Eve in the garden of Eden
2	Patriarchs	Burgundy	God's blood covenant with Abraham	God called Abraham and promised his children land, a royal kingdom, and worldwide blessing
3	Egypt & Exodus	Red	The Red Sea	God freed his people from slavery in Egypt so they could worship Him
4	Desert Wanderings	Tan	The color of the desert sands	God taught Israel to walk in faith through forty years of wandering in the desert
5	Conquest & Judges	Green	The green hills of Canaan	God led Israel into the Promised Land. They failed to teach their children and instead did what was right in their own eyes.
6	Royal Kingdom	Purple	Royalty	God established a kingdom on his servant David and promised him an eternal home

HOME STUDY: LOOKING AHEAD

The Royal Kingdom under David and Solomon is the high point of Israel's history. Flip over your chart and look at the next period. The black of the Divided Kingdom should warn you that there are dark times ahead.

King Solomon's son Rehoboam increases the oppressive policies of his father and the people revolt. The Kingdom divides into two separate kingdoms (Israel in the North and Judah to the South) and the kingdom of Israel is irrevocably changed.

The division of the Kingdom leads to idolatry and wickedness. Israel and Judah's spiritual separation from God leads to physical separation from their land in a period of foreign Exile.

• Use your chart to fill in the following information about these time periods:

Period name: <u>Divided Kingdom</u>   Time period: _____ 930 BC - 722 BC _____

Period color: ___ Black ___   Color meaning: ___ Israel's darkest days ___

The two kingdoms are represented on the chart by two horizontal bars: the Northern Kingdom of ___ Israel ___, its capital at ___ Samaria ___; and the Southern Kingdom of ___ Judah ___, its capital at ___ Jerusalem ___.

Color of names in Jesus' bloodline: ___ Red ___ (kings of Judah in the South)

Kings of the Northern Kingdom are printed in black. Do you recognize any names? What do you know about them, if anything? _____
Answers will vary. Ahab (husband of Jezebel) and Jehu are among those that may be recognized. That they are black suggests they are not in Jesus' blood line.

Many prophets spoke to the people of both kingdoms during this time. Their names are in italics and they are located near the kingdom to which they spoke. List any you have heard of and write down who they spoke to: Answers will vary.

What new world power rises during this time? ___ Assyria ___

Period name: <u>Exile</u>

Period color: ___ Baby Blue ___   Color meaning: ___ Judah "singing the blues" in "Baby-lon" ___

Time period: ___ 722 BC - 540 BC ___   New world power: ___ Babylon ___

List the three events found in the solid blue boxes: _____
Israel goes into exile; three deportations; seventy years of exile (Babylonian captivity)

This map properly belongs to the following period.
It is included here so that students can refer to it as they read about the Divided Kingdom.

• The readings for the period of the Divided Kingdom are complex due to the number of players and the way the story swings back and forth between events in Israel in the North and Judah in the South. Rather than reading through it, the following selections will focus you on the fact of and reason for the split and will give you a feeling for why and how the people then went into exile. Some readings from the prophets (supplemental books for this period) are included so you can hear God's cry of love for His disobedient children.

Divided Kingdom:

1 Kings 11:26–13:10; 14	The Royal Kingdom divides; sins of the North
Hosea 11,14	A message to the North (Israel; aka Ephraim)
Jeremiah 31:1-14	A message to the South (Judah)

Exile:

| 2 Kings 17 | Exile of the North (Israel) |
| 2 Kings 25:1-21 | Exile of the South (Judah) |

The Divided Kingdom
(930-586 B.C.)

PREPARING TO LEAD SESSION 6: DIVIDED KINGDOM, EXILE

- For this session only, read all instructions to leaders, preview the DVD, and familiarize yourself with all questions and responses.

- Carefully read the following Lesson Overview:

Lesson Overview
The glorious kingdom established under King David ruptures in Session 6 as a result of Solomon's sin. Jeff Cavins explains the state of Israel after Solomon's death and the way it soon divides into two separate kingdoms: the ten tribes to the North secede from David's throne and become a new tribe, still called Israel and run from the northern capital of Samaria; two tribes to the South remain loyal to David's successor and become the kingdom of Judah with its capital in Jerusalem, which houses the Temple and the Ark of the Covenant. A separate religion is established in the North and that kingdom quickly slides into apostasy. Jeff explains how to navigate this complicated period of many kings and prophets. Despite the messages the prophets bring both Israel and Judah to repent, they repeatedly turn from God.

Punishment inevitably comes in the form of exile. Israel falls to Assyria in 722 BC, is deported and scattered among the countries to the north. Judah hangs on a while longer but eventually is marched into Babylonian exile in 587 BC. Jerusalem and the Temple are destroyed. The period ends with all that is left of the old Israel—the tribe of Judah—waiting out seventy years of captivity far from home.

LEADING THE CLASS SESSION

STEP 1: Opening Review (fifteen minutes)
- Begin with a brief review of the previous lesson, referring to the Lesson Overview on page L-23 if needed. Ask what has been accomplished of God's original promises to Abraham?

- Introduce the two new periods by their colors and have everyone review all the periods on their beads. (Divided Kingdom is black for Israel's darkest period; Exile is baby blue because in it, Judah is "singing the blues" in "Baby-lon.")

- Read or present the Lesson Overview provided above in your own words.

- The many kings and prophets of the Divided Kingdom period can make it difficult to keep things straight when reading from this period in the Bible. Take time to review the Home Study questions on page 27 and make sure that everyone understands the way the kingdoms, kings, and prophets appear on The Bible Timeline chart. This will prove to be a helpful reference in the future as people read the story for themselves.

STEP 2: View DVD (thirty minutes)
The Student Workbook section for each lesson begins with a brief outline of Jeff Cavins' talk. Space is included for taking notes. Ask group members to write down at least one thing that stands out to them from the talk to share later with the class.

Divided Kingdom
Exile

Tyranny Leads to Division
God's People are Removed from the Promised Land

NOTES

1. Israel after the death of Solomon

[handwritten notes:] Solomon 2-years Built temple 13 yrs palace enslaved own people

[handwritten notes:] 10 tribes North Israel 2 south Judah

[handwritten notes:] Stepping into a very comfy Rot/part of bible

[handwritten notes:] Elizca Elisha

[handwritten notes:] Kings Workbook 35-36

[handwritten notes:] one vers 1 Ks 12 & 16 930 BC

2. God sends prophets to warn the people

3. Israel (the North) falls to Assyria

4. Judah (the South) is marched into Exile

[handwritten notes:] Exile: God physically moves you to where you "are" spiritually

[handwritten notes:] Why in exile: Law written so Isral finds on Oed of Egyt. As what happed to them (freedom) they are to do to others

1. Solomon's son Rehoboam, following the advice of his fellows instead of his father's advisors, refused to lighten the heavy load Solomon had laid on his subjects. In response, the ten tribes to the North denounced David's line and formed their own kingdom.

2. Northern Kingdom: <u>Israel</u>; Southern Kingdom: <u>Judah</u>

3. Worried that the people would return to Judah to worship at the Jerusalem Temple, Jeroboam set up golden calves at two cities and announced that these were the gods that brought Israel out of Egypt. He also appointed priests who were not Levites to service these altars. In effect, he started his own religion. It wasn't long before the people fell into idolatry and followed the wicked practices of their neighbors.

4. The Southern Kingdom (Judah) may have lasted longer than the Northern Kingdom (Israel) because God continued to be worshiped in the South, in the Jerusalem Temple, and David's royal line was on the throne there. All the kings of the South were from David's royal line. For the sake of His promise to David, God continued to "maintain a lamp" in Jerusalem—in other words, His Holy city and the promised throne were maintained. The people did not always obey and eventually even they were exiled, but the situation in the North was far worse. A succession of evil dynasties took the throne. Not one king followed God, in spite of many prophetic warnings and pleas.

   If there is time, introduce the charts on pages 34 and 35 of the workbook; these provide an overview of the kings of both kingdoms. You may want to get familiar with them yourself before you lead the discussion group.

5. By rejecting God's rule and following after other gods, the people of Israel and Judah removed themselves from God's presence. This spiritual exile was manifested physically when God removed them from the land He had chosen.

6. With the exception of 2 Chronicles, which contains a parallel history to the books of 1 and 2 Kings, the supplemental books during this period are written by prophets God sent with messages of love and warning to Judah and Israel (two, Obadiah and Jonah, carried messages to other nations).

   The chart of the prophets on page 36 can help people keep straight which prophet speaks when and to whom. Point it out for future reference.

DISCUSSION QUESTIONS

1. Shortly after Solomon's death, the glorious Royal Kingdom split in two. (Look at the map on page 28. The line of division is just North of Jerusalem.) What precipitated the division?

2. What were the two resulting kingdoms called?

   Northern Kingdom: _____ Southern Kingdom: _____

3. What grave sin did King Jeroboam commit soon after the Northern Kingdom was formed, and why?

4. Notice on your chart how much longer the Southern Kingdom lasted than the North. How do you account for this?

5. In what sense is the punishment Israel and Judah received for their sin a physical reflection of their spiritual state?

6. Read the names of the supplemental books up in the top portion of the chart during these periods. How many are there? ____18____ Who do you think wrote these books, and why did they write them?

7. Baby blue recalls the sorrow of the exiles as Judah spent seventy years "singing the blues" in "Baby-lon."

8. Ask someone to read Jeremiah 31:31-33: "Behold, the days are coming, says the LORD, when I will make a new covenant with the house of Israel and the house of Judah, not like the covenant which I made with their fathers when I took them by the hand to bring them out of the land of Egypt, my covenant which they broke, though I was their husband, says the LORD. But this is the covenant which I will make with the house of Israel after those days, says the LORD: I will put my law within them, and I will write it upon their hearts; and I will be their God, and they shall be my people."

   Jeremiah announces the new covenant that will be made in Jesus Christ. It will be made during the time period of Messianic Fulfillment.

9. Answers will vary; encourage discussion.

STEP 4: Closing
Gather discussion groups together for the close. Have each share one thing they learned or ask them together to comment on the significance of the period. If you haven't done so already, point out the three charts on pages 34–36 in the Student Workbook: "Kings of Israel," "Kings of Judah," and "Prophets," which are provided for later reference. Explain the home study assignment for the following week, which will be periods 9 and 10: Return and Maccabean Revolt. These are the final two periods in the Old Testament.

Prayer:
Lead participants in the Responsive Prayer found on page 46 of the Student Workbook or just pray the portion that applies to this lesson (see Closing Prayer on opposite page).

7. The dark period of the Divided Kingdom is fittingly represented by the color black. What color is used to help recall the period of Exile and why?

8. Read Jeremiah 31:31-33. God says that Israel has broken the covenant He made with Him. Look along the top of your chart where the covenant icons in "God's Family Plan" appear. What is this "new covenant" Jeremiah announces and when will it be made?

9. How might looking to "other gods" in our culture result in a spiritual exile from God? Search your heart to see if there are idolatrous attachments you need to forsake.

CLOSING PRAYER

God's plan unfolded through history and gives us the Story for our lives. Let us pray in the name of Jesus:

Israel split into rival kingdoms and fell into idolatry:

—Help us to choose your kingdom over other loves.

You punished first Israel, then Judah, with exile. Prophets brought a message of hope:

—In our exile due to sin, show us the way home.

Our Father…

HOME STUDY: LOOKING AHEAD

A small remnant of God's people return to the Promised Land after seventy years of punishment in exile. In the Return, they will work hard to rebuild what they lost through sin and idolatry.

After a number of generations, a new foreign power comes on the scene and the Jews are faced with a new threat. Will they succumb to a pagan culture and religion, or will they be faithful to God? The Maccabean Revolt tells this stirring story of faith and courage.

• Use your chart to fill in the following information about these time periods:

Period name: <u>Return</u> Time period: _____ 538 BC - 167 BC _____

Period color: ___ Yellow ___ Color meaning: ___ Judah returns to brighter days ___

Apart from the actual return to the land itself, what important activities characterized this time? (Read events 49, 50, and 52.)

___ Zerubbabel rebuilds the Temple ___   ___ Ezra returns and teaches ___

___ Nehemiah rebuilds the Jerusalem walls ___

Prophets during that time: ___ Haggai, Zechariah, and Malachi ___

Two new world powers: ___ Persia ___   ___ Greece ___

Concurrent people/events in secular history: _____

___ Plato, Socrates, Aristotle, Alexander the Great; The Septuagint; Great Wall of China built ___

Period name: <u>Maccabean Revolt</u> Time period: ___ 167 BC - 0 ___

Period color: ___ Orange ___ Color meaning: Fire in the oil lamps in the purified Temple

Two main events: Antiochus desecrates the Temple; purification of the Temple (Hannukah)

New world power: ___ Rome ___

Supplemental books: ___ 2 Maccabees, Wisdom of Solomon, and Sirach ___

continued

• Read the following selections to get a summary of the periods of Return and Maccabean Revolt.

Return:

Ezra 1,3	Cyrus foretold; Return; Foundations of the Temple laid
Ezra 4–6	Samaritan opposition
Nehemiah 1, 2, 6	Nehemiah's return; rebuilding of Jerusalem walls

Maccabean Revolt:

1 Maccabees 1, 2	Maccabean revolt
2 Maccabees 7	Seven martyrs and their mother

The Kings of Israel and Kings of Judah charts on pages 34 and 35 name every king of those kingdom; tell when and for how long they reigned, whether they were bad or good kings (i.e., whether they followed God), and the relationship of each to his predecessor; and present the manner of their death.

Review the features of these charts with the participants in your group. In the Kings of Israel chart (on the facing page) point out the string of bad kings and the events that ended their reigns. The alternating gray and white blocks indicate the frequent changes of dynasty (royal family). Be sure to note how the Southern Kingdom (i.e., Judah) differs.

KINGS OF ISRAEL (NORTHERN KINGDOM)
930-722 BC: Nine Dynasties*

No.	King	Date BC	Bad/ Good	Years Reigned	Relation to Predecessor	End of Reign	Scripture Reference
1	Jeroboam I	930-909	B	22		Stricken by God	1 Kg 11:26-14:20
2	Nadab	909-908	B	2	Son	Killed by Baasha	1 Kg 15:25-28
3	Baasha	908-886	B	24	Son of Ahijah	Died	1 Kg 15:16-16:7
4	Elah	886-885	B	2	Son	Killed by Zimri	1 Kg 16:6-14
5	Zimri	885	B	7 days	Captain of Chariot	Suicide by Fire	1 Kg 16:9-20
6	(Tibni)*	885-880	B	7	Son of Ginath	Died	1 Kg 16:21-22
7	Omri	885-874	B	12	Captain of Army	Died	1 Kg 16:23-28
8	Ahab	874-853	B	22	Son	Wounded in Battle	1 Kg 16:28-22:40
9	Ahaziah	853-852	B	2	Son	Fell to His Death	1Kg 22:40-2 Kg 1:18
10	Joram	852-841	B	12	Brother	Killed by Jehu	2 Kg 3:1-9:25
11	Jehu	841-814	B	28	(none)	Died	2 Kg 9:1-10:36
12	Jehoahaz	814-798	B	17	Son	Died	2 Kg 13:1-9
13	Jehoash	798-782	B	16	Son	Died	2 Kg 13:10-14:16
14	Jeroboam II	793-753	B	41	Son	Died	2 Kg 14:23-29
15	Zechariah	753	B	6 months	Son	Killed by Shallum	2 Kg 14:29-15:12
16	Shallum	752	B	1 month	(none)	Killed by Menahem	2 Kg 15:10-15
17	Menahem	752-742	B	10	(none)	Died	2 Kg 15:15-22
18	Pekahiah	742-740	B	2	Son	Killed by Pekah	2 Kg 15:22-26
19	Pekah	740-732	B	20	Captain of Army	Killed by Hoshea	2 Kg 15:27-31
20	Hoshea	732-722	B	9	(none)	Exile to Assyria	2 Kg 15:30-17

* Shading indicates divisions between the nine dynasties that ruled the Northern Kingdom. Tibni, who unsuccessfully contended with Omri for the throne after Zimri's death, does not count as a separate dynasty. His name is in the chart because his reign is mentioned in the Bible, and he is included in some lists of kings of Israel.

KINGS OF JUDAH (SOUTHERN KINGDOM)
930-586 BC: One Dynasty

No.	King	Date BC	Bad/Good	Years Reigned	Relation to Predecessor	End of Reign	Scripture Reference
1	Rehoboam I	930-913	B	17	Son of Solomon	Died	1 Kg 11:42-14:31
2	Abijah	913-910	B	3	Son	Died	1 Kg 14:31-15:8
3	Asa	910-869	G	41	Son	Died	1 Kg 15:8-24
4	Jehoshaphat	872-848	G	25	Son	Died	1 Kg 22:41-55
5	Jehoram	848-841	B	8	Son	Stricken by God	2 Kg 8:16-24
6	Ahaziah	841	B	1	Son	Killed by Jehu	2 Kg 8:24-9:29
7	Athaliah	841-835	B	7	Mother	Killed by Army	2 Kg 11:1-20
8	Joash	835-796	G	40	Grandson	Killed by Servants	2 Kg 11:1-12:21
9	Amaziah	796-767	G	29	Son	Killed by Court	2 Kg 14:1-20
10	Uzziah	792-740	G	52	Son	Stricken by God	2 Kg 15:1-7
11	Jotham	750-732	G	16	Son	Died	2 Kg 15:32-38
12	Ahaz	735-715	B	16	Son	Died	2 Kg 16:1-20
13	Hezekiah	715-686	G	29	Son	Died	2 Kg 18:1-20:21
14	Manasseh	697-642	B	55	Son	Died	2 Kg 21:1-18
15	Amon	642-640	B	2	Son	Killed by Servants	2 Kg 21:19-26
16	Josiah	640-609	G	31	Son	Wounded in Battle	2 Kg 22:1-23:30
17	Johoahaz	609	B	3 Months	Son	Exiled to Egypt	2 Kg 23:31-33
18	Jehoiakim	609-598	B	11	Brother	Died in Seige	2 Kg 23:34-24:5
19	Jehoiachin	598-597	B	3 Months	Son	Exiled to Babylon	2 Kg 24:6-16
20	Zedekiah	597-586	B	11	Uncle	Exiled to Babylon	2 Kg 24:17-25:30

The Prophets of the Northern and Southern Kingdoms chart (on the facing page) lists all of the prophets, when each prophesies, and whether their prophesying was before, during, or after Judah's exile to Babylon. It also indicates the audience of each prophet and what country was then in power.

PROPHETS OF THE
NORTHERN & SOUTHERN KINGDOMS
870-424 BC

No.	Prophet	Date BC	Pre/Post Exile	Audience	World Ruler	Scripture Reference
1	Elijah	870	Pre Exile	Israel	Assyria	1 Kg 17-2 Kg 2:15
2	Elisha	850	Pre Exile	Israel	Assyria	1 Kg 19:1-2 Kg 13:21
3	Obadiah	848-841	Pre Exile	Edom	Assyria	2 Kg 8:16-24; 2 Chron. 21:1-20 *
4	Joel	840	Pre Exile	Judah	Assyria	2 Kg 12:1-21; 2 Chron. 24:1-27 *
5	Jonah	800-753	Pre Exile	Assyria	Assyria	2 Kg 13:10-25; 14:23-29 *
6	Amos	760-753	Pre Exile	Israel	Assyria	2 Kg 14:23-15:7 *
7	Hosea	750-715	Pre Exile	Israel	Assyria	2 Kg 14:23-18:12 *
8	Isaiah	740-680	Pre Exile	Judah	Assyria	2 Kg 15:1-20:21; 2 Chron. 26:16-32:33 *
9	Micah	735-700	Pre Exile	Judah	Assyria	2 Kg 15:32-19:37; 2 Chron. 27:1-32:23 *
10	Zephaniah	632-628	Pre Exile	Judah	Assyria	2 Kg 22:1-2; 2 Chron. 34:1-7 *
11	Nahum	664-654	Pre Exile	Assyria	Assyria	2 Kg 21:1-18; 2 Chron. 33:1-20 *
12	Jeremiah	625-580	Pre Exile	Judah	Assyria/Babylon	2 Kg 22:3-25:30; 2 Chron. 34:1-36:21 *
13	Habakkuk	610-605	Pre Exile	Judah	Babylon	2 Kg 23:31-24:7; 2 Chron. 36:1-8 *
14	Baruch	600	Exile	Judah	Babylon	2 Kg 24:8-25:30; 2 Chron. 36:9-21 *
15	Daniel	605-535	Exile	Exiles	Babylon/Persia	2 Kg 23:34-25:30; 2 Chron. 36:4-23 *
16	Ezekiel	590-571	Exile	Exiles	Babylon	2 Kg 24:8-25:30; 2 Chron. 36:9-21 *
17	Haggai	520	Post Exile	Judah	Persia	Ezra 5:1-6:15 *
18	Zechariah	520-480	Post Exile	Judah	Persia	Ezra 5:1-6:15 *
19	Malachi	432-424	Post Exile	Judah	Persia	Ezra 5:1-6:15 *

* These prophets also have Old Testament books named after them.

PREPARING TO LEAD SESSION 7: THE RETURN, THE MACCABEAN REVOLT

- *For this session only, read all instructions to leaders, preview the DVD, and familiarize yourself with all questions and responses.*

- *Carefully read the following Lesson Overview:*

Lesson Overview

The exiles from Judah return to the Land in session 7, chastened and ready to rebuild not just their land but their lives as well. Jeff Cavins explains how the return occurs in three waves that start when King Cyrus of Persia sends them home to rebuild the Temple in 537 BC. Zerubbabel, a man in David's line, leads this first effort. Following him are Ezra, who teaches the people, and Nehemiah, who heads the rebuilding of the Jerusalem walls. Obstacles to building will be explained, and the way God helps them to triumph.

The Jews are essentially faithful to God during the period of the Return, but the rise of Greek influence threatens their identity and eventually their lives. When Antiochus Ephiphanes desecrates the Temple and tries to force the Jews to abandon their faith, they revolt. Led by Judas Maccabeus and his sons, they enter a period of self-rule that ends after Rome rises to power.

LEADING THE CLASS SESSION

STEP 1: Opening Review (fifteen minutes)
- *Begin with a brief overview of the previous lesson (see the Lesson Overview on page L-29) and explain the Divided Kingdom section on the chart to anyone who missed it.*

- *Introduce the two new periods by their colors (the Return is yellow, as Judah returns to brighter days; the Maccabean Revolt is remembered by orange, which represents the flame in the lamps in the purified Temple). Use the Lesson Overview above to help you summarize these two periods.*

- *Have everyone review the periods on their beads. This is the last period in the Old Testament. Can anyone recite all the periods, colors, and meanings using the beads?*

Memory Tip: *You can remember the progression of world powers by this phrase built from the first letters of their names: Eat A Big Purple GRape (E=Egypt, A=Assyria, B=Babylon, G=Greece, R=Rome).*

STEP 2: View DVD (thirty minutes)
The Student Workbook section for each lesson begins with a brief outline of Jeff Cavins' talk. Space is included for taking notes. Ask group members to write down at least one thing that stands out to them from the talk to share later with the class.

The Return
The Maccabean Revolt

Judah Returns to the Promised Land
Faithful Jews Fight to Preserve their Identity

NOTES

1. The Exiles Return to the Land

   • 537 BC – Zerubbabel returns and rebuilds the Temple

   • 458 BC – Ezra returns and teaches

   • 444 BC – Nehemiah returns and rebuilds the Jerusalem walls

2. Obstacles to Rebuilding

3. The Rise of Greek Influence

4. The Jews Revolt

STEP 3: *Small group discussion (thirty minutes)*

These questions for group discussion pertain to the taped lecture for Session 7. Suggested responses are given below to help facilitators guide the discussion. Get the discussion started by asking: "What stood out to you in the DVD and why?" Ask students to share something memorable they wrote down while listening to Jeff Cavins' talk.

1. The Return is characterized by the color yellow, representing brighter days as Judah returns to the land of Canaan after seventy years of exile.

2. God called on a foreign king, Cyrus of Persia, who was "stirred up by the Lord" to send back anyone who wants to return to Judah to live and to rebuild the Temple. Everyone who stays behind is told to help with silver, gold, and other freewill offerings. Cyrus provides building materials and returns the Temple treasure previously stolen by Nebuchadnezzar of Babylon.

   The prophet Isaiah had foretold this very event many years previously, with exact detail right down to Cyrus' name.

3. Everything had been lost. The Jews had to rebuild the Temple, the city itself, and their lives. This latter included instruction in God's Law. Each "return" tackled a different aspect of this rebuilding (see the event boxes on the chart).

4. Judah faced opposition from within and without on their return to Canaan. From the start, they were opposed by the Samaritans, who consider them a political threat. The Samaritans provide opposition every step of the way. From the inside, the rebuilding effort is compromised when the people stop working on the Temple in order to build their own homes. Later on, the Jewish leaders put heavy taxes on the common people to the point that they have to pawn their fields and houses and even their children. They overcome these obstacles of sin with the help of Haggai and Nehemiah, who called them to account and led reforms. Thanks to the ongoing and dedicated leadership of Ezra and Nehemiah, the community was established and brought under the rule of God's law.

5. A policy of radical Hellenization threatened their Jewish identity. The Greeks—Antiochus Epiphanes in particular—imposed the worship of their gods and banned under penalty of death not just worship but all practices that separated the Jews from others (the Sabbath, circumcision, etc.). Many were being killed until a man named Mattathias and his sons stood up against them and launched an all-out campaign to fight for their faith. Ultimately, they were successful in pushing back the Greeks and maintained their own rule for a time.

6. Rather than conforming to Greek ways and abandoning their religion, many of the Jews resisted and fought back, risking their lives in the process. 1 and 2 Maccabees are full of heroic stories of resistance and martyrs. Clearly they have learned the lessons of the exile and would rather follow God than abandon Him.

DISCUSSION QUESTIONS

1. What color is used to characterize the Return, and why?

2. What unlikely person did God use to return His people to the Promised Land, and how?

3. What three kinds of rebuilding were necessary when the Jews returned?

4. What kinds of opposition did they face, and how did they overcome them?

5. What kind of crisis confronted the Jews at the beginning of the Maccabean period, when Greece became the world power?

6. Based on the story of the Maccabees, what evidence do you see that Israel is learning to trust God?

7. The catalyst for the Maccabean Revolt was the desecration of the Temple by Antiochus Epiphanes, and the war started by the courageous Mattathias led three years later to the taking back of the Temple and its purification. According to the Talmud, oil enough for one lamp lasted miraculously eight days. The event is commemorated today as Hanukah—the Festival of Lights. The miracle of the oil, while not recorded in Scripture, gives us our color for this period: orange, for the light in the lamps.

8. Answers will vary. Are there any parallels between the Hellenization that threatened the identity of the Jews and secularism today?

9. One way to look at this question is to see what has been fulfilled of God's covenant with Abraham. He has had many descendants; they have inherited and inhabited the promised land of Canaan, lost it and returned. They did become a royal kingdom but are now under foreign rule. It has been hundreds of years since someone in David's line has sat on the throne. The promise of worldwide blessing was fulfilled in a limited sense in Egypt, when Joseph saved many nations from starvation, and again under David and Solomon, but this promise seems to have foundered.

    Another way to look at it is to follow the "God's Family Plan" icons on the chart: what began with a covenant relationship with a couple, Adam and Eve, grew to a family with Noah and his wife and sons, a tribe under Abraham, a nation under Moses, and a kingdom under David. Great progress has been made and yet something still separates God from His children.

10. There remains the problem of sin: man's fallen nature still separates him from God. Even with all the benefits and advice and help God has given them, Israel can't seem to follow Him as He asks.

    There also remains the problem of the broken covenant. This is a problem: how can God pay out the terms of the covenant, which demand death for the guilty party, and at the same time keep His promises?

    How will God move to solve these two things?

STEP 4: Closing
Gather discussion groups together for the close. Have each share one thing they learned or ask them together to comment on the significance of the periods.

(continued on next page)

7. Why is the color orange used to represent the period of the Maccabean Revolt?

8. What have you learned from these two periods that you can apply to your own life?

9. We have completed the Old Testament story. What positive progress has been made in God's plan to restore His children to Himself?

10. What is left to be done?

CLOSING PRAYER

God's plan unfolded through history and gives us the Story for our lives. Let us pray in the name of Jesus:

You brought the exiles home; they rebuilt the Temple and Jerusalem and were taught once more from your law:

—Rebuild our broken hearts and lives as we return to you.

The Maccabees stood up against the threats of Hellenization:

—Help us resist worldliness in our culture and follow only you.

Our Father…

Explain the Home Study assignment for the following and final week, which will be the two New Testament periods, 11 and 12: Messianic Fulfillment and The Church. Because we have come to the end of the Old Testament, another review of the periods follows the usual preparation.

Prayer:
Lead participants in the Responsive Prayer found on page 46 of the Student Workbook or just pray the portion that applies to this lesson.

HOME STUDY: LOOKING AHEAD

The Old Testament is finished, and the time for fulfillment of God's promises has come! God's people have been waiting for the Messiah for centuries and the long years of spiritual exile end at last in the period of Messianic Fulfillment. Will the Jews recognize the Son of Man and the Kingdom He has come to establish on Earth?

At the close of His earthly ministry Jesus commissions His apostles to spread the message of salvation to the ends of the earth. The seed of Abraham, bearing fruit in the Church, will now become a blessing to the world.

• Use your chart to fill in the following information about these time periods:

Period name: <u>Messianic Fulfillment</u>   Time period: _____ 0 - 33 AD _____

Period color: _____ Gold _____   Color meaning: _____ The gifts of the Magi _____

Narrative book: ___ Luke ___   Supplemental books: ___ Matthew, Mark, and John ___

(Note: The four Gospels are of equal importance; the narrative book was chosen from among the synoptics because it includes the infancy narrative and therefore provides a more complete story of the history covered in the Bible Timeline.)

Period name: <u>The Church</u>   Time period: _____ 33 AD - Present _____

Period color: _____ White _____   Color meaning: _____ The spotless bride of Christ _____

Name the three "waves of witness" that form the structure of this period:

_____ Witness in Jerusalem _____   _____ Witness in Judea and Samaria _____

_____ Witness to the ends of the Earth _____

• You may already be familiar with the Gospels and Acts of the Apostles, which tell the story of the two final periods in the Bible Timeline. It is difficult to pull just a few representative passages from them. To prepare for the lesson on Messianic Fulfillment and the Church, you might choose from among the following readings.

Messianic Fulfillment:

Luke 1–4	The announcement and birth and temptation of the Messiah
Luke 6:12–36	The Twelve Apostles; "Sermon on the Plain"
Luke 9:1–36	Sending out the Twelve; feeding the 5,000; Peter's confession of Christ; the Transfiguration
Luke 22–24	Last Supper, Passion, Resurrection

The Church:

Acts 2	Pentecost
Acts 7–8	Stephen's martyrdom; the message begins to spread
Acts 9–11	Saul's conversion; Peter's vision

Please turn the page for *Home Study: Review.*

HOME STUDY: REVIEW

- Using your memory bead wristband, review once more the names and color meanings of the Old Testament periods. Have you memorized the colors yet? Complete the list that you started on page 26:

	Period Name	Color	Meaning	Phrase
7	Divided Kingdom	Black	Israel's darkest period	Israel split into rival kingdoms and fell into idolatry
8	Exile	Baby Blue	"Singing the Blues" in "Baby-lon"	God punished first Israel, then Judah, with exile. Prophets brought a message of hope
9	Return	Yellow	Judah returning home to brighter days	God brought the exiles back to Canaan; they rebuilt the Temple and Jerusalem and were taught once more from the Law
10	Maccabean Revolt	Orange	Fire in the Oil lamps in the purified Temple	Mattathias and his sons stood up against the threats of Hellenization
11	Messianic Fulfillment	Gold	Gifts of the Magi	God sent His only Son, Jesus Christ the Messiah, to fulfill all His promises
12	The Church	White	The spotless bride of Christ	The Church carries on God's work in the world

PREPARING TO LEAD SESSION 8: MESSIANIC FULFILLMENT, THE CHURCH

- *For this session only, read all instructions to leaders, preview the DVD, and familiarize yourself with all questions and responses.*

- *Carefully read the following Lesson Overview:*

Lesson Overview

All God's promises reach their fulfillment in the New Covenant of Jesus Christ in Session 8. Jeff Cavins looks at the coming of the promised Messiah, who is God with us, come as a man to fulfill all righteousness. He answers the question asked in the Garden of Eden: "Is anybody going to trust God completely?" Jesus trusts the Father to the death. He is the New Israel; the New Moses; He leads people in a New Exodus and a new Return from Exile, and He gives them a New Law. He reconstitutes the scattered twelve tribes of Israel around Himself and establishes the New Kingdom, which is built on the twelve apostles. He is the Lamb of God who comes to take away the sins of the world. In His passion and death, He takes upon himself the curses of the broken covenant. In His death and resurrection, this Seed of the Woman crushes the head of the Serpent. The new life that is possible in Him restores the family relationship with God that was broken at the Fall. In Christ, Christians are adopted as children of God. The entire story has been pointing to this.

In the final period, Jeff shows how Christ lives on after His ascension through His Church. The Gospel is proclaimed first in Jerusalem, then in Judea and Samaria and finally to the ends of the earth. God's kingdom is opened to all people who believe. The book of Acts is presented as a narrative that provides a framework for reading the rest of the New Testament. The story that began in the Garden of Eden extends through the lives of all Christians in the Church, through each one of us. It is our story; this is our family history. And the same question faces us as has faced everyone since Adam. Can you trust God? Jeff challenges each one of us to take up the baton and continue the part of the story that is ours.

LEADING THE CLASS SESSION

STEP 1: Opening Review (fifteen minutes)
- *Begin this lesson with a brief recap of the story as it is told in the Old Testament. One way to do this might be to ask ten people in turn to characterize a period in a few sentences, beginning with Early World. Refer to the Lesson Overviews or the Responsive Prayer (p. 46) as needed.*

- *Review the sequence of periods using the memory bead wristbands. Introduce the final two, from the New Testament:* Gold *(Messianic Fulfillment) is the color of the gifts of the Magi, of kingship.* White *represents the spotless bride of Christ, which is The Church. Even though in the Bible this covers less than a century, the period of the Church continues today. Use the Lesson Overview above to explain what this final lesson will cover.*

STEP 2: View DVD (thirty minutes)
The Student Workbook section for each lesson begins with a brief outline of Jeff Cavins' talk. Space is included for taking notes. Ask group members to write down at least one thing that stands out to them from the talk to share later with the class.

Literal
1 *allegorical — relate to Kt*
2 *moral — relate to my life*
3 *anagogical — future*

Cristo Centric

hypostatic Union

NOTES

1. The Coming of the Promised Messiah

10 of Nisan
I found no fault
14 3pm jesus dies at
same time sacrificial
flock

Eliakim — Is 22
Prime Minister
Papa

heart of jesus ministry
release / forgive 70×7

2. Christ Lives on through His Church

Power when HS comes
to ends of earth — He ascends

Acts 1:8 — 8:3   Disciples
8:4 — 12:25   Community   Judea Samaria
12:25 — end   Church

Revelation 12
deceiver thrown down
Rome

Hypostatic union

STEP 3: Small group discussion (forty minutes)

These questions for group discussion pertain to the taped lecture for Session 8. Suggested responses are given below to help facilitators guide the discussion. Get the discussion started by asking: "What stood out to you in the DVD and why?" Ask students to share something memorable they wrote down while listening to Jeff Cavins' talk.

1. "The book of the genealogy of Jesus Christ, the son of David, the son of Abraham"—a son of David has finally come to sit on the throne! Participants may have personal reactions as well.

2. Jesus and His New Covenant fulfill the Old Covenant promises:

   • Jesus is the seed (child) of Mary, the second Eve, who comes to defeat Satan, the Serpent, on the Cross. The original promise was given in the Early World to Adam and Eve after the Fall in the context of God's curse on the Serpent (Genesis 3:15).

   • Jesus Christ is the ultimate Passover Lamb who takes the place of all the others and makes the one sacrifice needed to atone for sin. We have been looking for the lamb since the Patriarchs and Genesis 22, when Abraham told Isaac that God would provide the lamb for the sacrifice.

   • The original promise came to Abraham in the Patriarchs period, in Genesis 12, 15, 17, and 22, and it referred to the descendants of Abraham. In Jesus this is a spiritual kingdom, the kingdom of God on Earth; in time that will find its ultimate fulfillment in the kingdom of God in heaven. The promise is not just for the blood descendants of Abraham but for all who are his children by faith.

   • Jesus Christ rules from the heavenly throne over a kingdom established on the twelve tribes and twelve apostles, successor to the kingdom of David. The original promise of David's everlasting throne was made in 2 Samuel 7 (Royal Kingdom).

   • Through her son Jesus Christ, Israel blessed the entire world and gave a way to all God's scattered children to return to Him. This was originally part of God's covenant promise to Abraham (Patriarchs; Genesis 12, 15, 17, 22)

3. Both Adam and Jesus were tested in a garden. While Adam was silent in the face of the Serpent's temptation and Eve's indecision, Jesus cried out to the Father. He defended his Bride and willingly suffered and laid down his life for her. He did the will of the Father. He trusted completely in God.

   By taking the fruit of the forbidden tree, Adam said, "my will be done." Jesus refused the fruit offered by Satan in the desert and drank of the cup of suffering instead. His entire life testifies "not my will, but Thine be done."

4. Gold (Messianic Fulfillment) is the color of the gifts of the Magi, of kingship. White represents the spotless bride of Christ, which is the Church. Just as the white of light contains all the colors of the rainbow and turns them into a pure, illuminating stream, the white of the Church gathers up all the colors of the previous periods and shows them in their full glory. All those other "colors" point toward and have their end in Christ and in His Church.

DISCUSSION QUESTIONS

1. Open to the very first book of the New Testament, Matthew, and read the first verse. Imagine you are a first-century Jew who knows the Story. What does this verse mean to you?

2. How do Jesus and His New Covenant fulfill these Old Covenant promises? (There are many; these are just a few)

   (*"Extra credit": Can you name the period and/or books of the Bible that tell about each of these promises, or explain the context in which it was given?*)

   • The seed of the woman will crush the head of the serpent

   • God will provide a lamb for the sacrifice

   • God's people will have a land/nation/kingdom to live in

   • That kingdom will be ruled by someone sitting on David's everlasting throne

   • Israel will be a source of blessing to the entire world

3. What did Jesus do, that Adam failed to do?

4. Explain the meanings of the colors used to represent Messianic Fulfillment and the Church.

5. Christ lives on in the Church through the Holy Spirit, which lives in the hearts of Christian believers and which animates and unifies the Body of Christ, the Church.

6. The Gospel message was preached first in Jerusalem. Persecution pushed the believers out to witness in Judea and Samaria. From there, they took the message out to the ends of the Earth. This process is described at the beginning of Acts (1:8) and provides a structure for that book.

7. & 8. Encourage discussion of both questions.

STEP 4: Closing
Gather discussion groups together for the close. Have each share the most important thing they learned in this study or what they will do with what they have learned.

Before you close, point out the sections at the close of the workbook, in particular the one called "Continuing the Journey" (p. 47). This will explain a number of ways people can take what they've learned and put it into practice. Show people the reading plan on page 48 and encourage them to read through the fourteen narrative books for themselves. Finally, the "Narrative and Supplemental Books" chart on page 49 is a handy reference tool for seeing how the remaining books of the Bible fit into the fourteen that form the narrative structure.

Prayer:
Lead participants in the Responsive Prayer found on page 46 of the Student Workbook or just pray the portion that applies to this lesson (see Closing Prayer on opposite page).

5. After Christ's death and Resurrection, how was He able to live on, both in and with the Church?

6. Describe the "three waves of witness" that propelled the gospel message outward from Jerusalem.

7. How do you live the life of Christ today?

8. Israel's story is our story. What difference does knowing the Story make in your life?

CLOSING PRAYER

God's plan unfolded through history and gives us the Story for our lives. Let us pray in the name of Jesus:

You sent your only Son, Jesus Christ the Messiah, to fulfill all your promises:

– Give us new life in Him.

The Church carries on your work in the world:

– Make us faithful ambassadors of your love.

Our Father…

Close all but the first lesson with a responsive reading of this prayer, reading up through the period you have just learned about. (Alternatively, you may choose to pray just the piece related to the period you are studying. These are written into Step 4 under "Prayer" at the end of each lesson.) Over time, praying this will help people remember the character of each period and the flow of the story.

Pray the prayer in a way that is most comfortable for your group. Here is one suggestion:

Opening

Leader:	Read "God's plan unfolded through history ..."
All:	Speak to us as we read your word.

On each bead

Leader:	First line (describes the period)
Take turns:	Second line (a prayer specific to that period)
All:	Speak to us as we read your word.

Closing

All:	Our Father ...

If time is limited, on each bead you might take turns reading the first line, with everyone responding on the second line and omitting the general response.

RESPONSIVE PRAYER

Pray this Responsive Prayer with your groups, reading up to and including the period you are studying each week, to help you learn the periods and take them to heart. Later you can pray it on your own, using the memory bead wristband as a guide.

God's plan unfolded through history and gives us the Story for our lives. Let us pray in the name of Jesus:

R: *Speak to us as we read your Word!*

In the Early World, you created the heavens and Earth and tested Adam and Eve in the garden:

R. *Help us to always choose the life that you offer.*

In the time of the Patriarchs, you called Abraham and promised his children land, a royal kingdom, and worldwide blessing:

R. *Help us to always hope in your promises.*

You freed your people from slavery in Egypt so they could worship you:

R. *Free us from sin so we can serve and worship.*

You taught Israel to walk in faith through forty years wandering in the desert:

R. *Help us to trust in you, O God.*

You led Israel triumphantly into the Promised Land. They failed to teach their children and instead did what was right in their own eyes:

R. *Help us to keep our eyes on you and bring up our children in your way.*

You established a kingdom on your servant David and promised him an eternal throne:

R. *Establish your kingdom in our midst.*

Israel split into rival kingdoms and fell into idolatry:

R. *Help us to choose your kingship over other loves.*

You punished first Israel, then Judah, with exile. Prophets brought a message of hope:

R. *In our exile due to sin, show us the way home.*

You brought the exiles back to Canaan; they rebuilt the Temple and Jerusalem and were taught once more from your Law:

R. *Rebuild our broken hearts and lives as we return to you.*

Mattathais and his sons stood up against the threats of Hellenization:

R. *Help us resist worldiness in our culture and follow only you.*

You sent your only Son, Jesus Christ the Messiah, to fulfill all your promises:

R. *Give us new life in him.*

The Church carries on your work in the world:

R. *Make us faithful ambassadors of your love.*

Our Father…

CONTINUING THE JOURNEY

- If you ever want a quick review of the Story, turn to Acts 7 and read the way Stephen defended his belief in Christ as the Son of God (to the Sanhedrin, before he was stoned and became the first Christian martyr).

- Reinforce what you have learned by continuing to memorize the twelve periods and reviewing the key people and events of each. Use the *Bible Timeline* chart as a guide.

- Start reading the Story for yourself! The first time through, stick to the narrative books. Later, start reading the others in context of the appropriate period and narrative book. Keep your *Bible Timeline* chart and bookmark in your Bible so you can refer to them.

  The reading guide on the next page can be used to track your progress through the fourteen narrative books. By reading four chapters a day, you will read through the entire Story in about three months.

- Once you have a good grasp of the story, you might read at a much slower pace so you can dig in and meditate on what God is saying to you. Try to make Scripture reading—even if it is only for a few moments—a part of your daily routine.

- It might be helpful to keep a journal as you read. Each day, write what you read followed by two things: what the passage says, and what it says to you. Pray first, listen during, and offer up a response to God. *The Bible Timeline Guided Journal* can help you read through the fourteen narrative books in this way.

Blessings on you as you continue The Great Adventure!

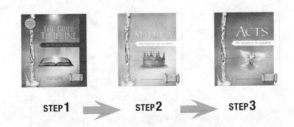

STEP 1 → STEP 2 → STEP 3

Now that people have the "big picture" of the Bible story, encourage them to immerse themselves in the story itself firsthand. This reading plan will take them through all fourteen narrative books of The Bible Timeline *at an average of four chapters per day over a ninety-day period.*

The Bible Timeline Guided Journal can help guide people through this process. In the Guided Journal, the readings for each period begin with an introduction that summarizes the period and lists the key people and events. The Journal contains a two-page spread for each day's reading assignment. Space is included to record items to remember about the reading, to keep track of questions for later study, and to respond to God in prayer. For each day there are reading hints, definitions, and questions that point to highlights of the reading and draw readers deeper into understanding the story.

Reading Through the Bible Historically
90-Day Reading Plan

Month #1

Early World
__ 1. Gen. 1-4
__ 2. Gen. 5-8
__ 3. Gen. 9-11

Patriarchs
__4. Gen. 12-16
__5. Gen. 17-20
__6. Gen. 21-24
__7. Gen. 25-28
__8. Gen. 29-32

__9. Gen. 33-36
__10. Gen. 37-40
__11. Gen. 41-45
__12. Gen. 46-50

Egypt and Exodus
__13. Ex. 1-4
__14. Ex. 5-8
__15. Ex. 9-12
__16. Ex. 13-16
__17. Ex. 17-20

__18. Ex. 21-24
__19. Ex. 25-28
__20. Ex. 29-32
__21. Ex. 33-36
__22. Ex. 37-40

Desert Wanderings
__23. Num. 1-4
__24. Num. 5-8
__25. Num. 9-12
__26. Num. 13-16

__27. Num. 17-20
__28. Num. 21-24
__29. Num. 25-28
__30. Num. 29-32
__31. Num. 33-36

Month #2

Conquest and Judges
__32. Josh. 1-4
__33. Josh. 5-8
__34. Josh. 9-12
__35. Josh. 13-16
__36. Josh. 17-20
__37. Josh. 21-24
__38. Judg. 1-4
__39. Judg. 5-8
__40. Judg. 9-12
__41. Judg. 13-16

__42. Judg. 17-21
__43. 1 Sam. 1-4
__44. 1 Sam. 5-8

Royal Kingdom
__45. 1 Sam. 9-12
__46. 1 Sam. 13-16
__47 1 Sam. 17-20
__48. 1 Sam. 21-24
__49. 1 Sam. 25-28
__50. 1 Sam. 29-31

__51. II Sam. 1-4
__52. II Sam. 5-8
__53. II Sam. 9-12
__54. II Sam. 13-16
__55. II Sam. 17-20
__56. II Sam. 21-24

__57. I Kings 1-4
__58. I Kings 5-8
__59. I Kings 9-11

Month #3

Divided Kingdom
__60. I Kings 12-15
__61. I Kings 16-19
__62. I Kings 20-22

__63. II Kings 1-4
__64. II Kings 5-8
__65. II Kings 9-12
__66. II Kings 13-16

Exile
__67. II Kings 17-20
__68. II Kings 21-25

Return
__69. Ezra 1-5

__70. Ezra 6-10
__71. Neh. 1-4
__72. Neh. 5-8
__73. Neh. 9-13

Maccabean Revolt
__74. 1 Macc. 1-4
__75. 1 Macc. 5-8
__76. 1 Macc. 9-12
__77. 1 Macc. 13-16

Messianic Fulfillment
__78. Luke 1-4
__79. Luke 5-8
__80. Luke 9-12
__81. Luke 13-16

__82. Luke 17-20
__83. Luke 21-24

Church
__84. Acts 1-4
__85. Acts 5-8
__86. Acts 9-12
__87. Acts 13-16
__88. Acts 17-20
__89. Acts 21-24
__90. Acts 25-28

This Narrative and Supplemental Books *diagram illustrates the way the fourteen narrative books correspond to the twelve periods of salvation history and shows at a glance how the Supplemental Books fit into the context of those periods and books.*

NARRATIVE AND SUPPLEMENTAL BOOKS

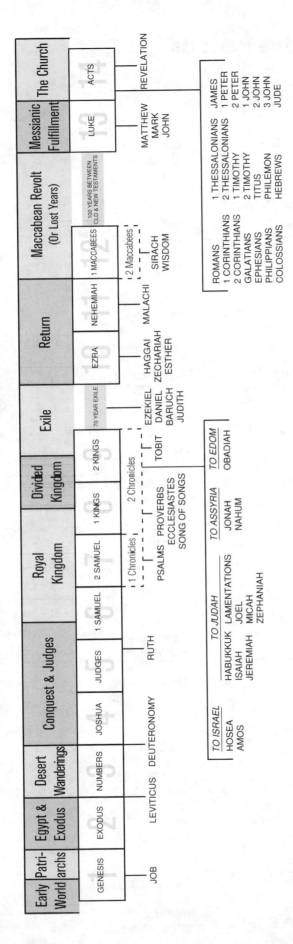

Early World	Patri-archs	Egypt & Exodus	Desert Wanderings	Conquest & Judges	Royal Kingdom	Divided Kingdom	Exile	Return	Maccabean Revolt (Or Lost Years)	Messianic Fulfillment	The Church

GENESIS — 1
EXODUS — 2
LEVITICUS   DEUTERONOMY
NUMBERS — 3
JOSHUA — 4
JUDGES — 5
RUTH
JOB
1 SAMUEL — 6
2 SAMUEL — 7
1 Chronicles
PSALMS   PROVERBS
ECCLESIASTES
SONG OF SONGS
1 KINGS — 8
2 KINGS — 9
2 Chronicles
TO ISRAEL
HOSEA
AMOS
TO JUDAH
HABUKKUK   LAMENTATIONS
ISAIAH   JOEL
JEREMIAH   MICAH
ZEPHANIAH
TO ASSYRIA
JONAH
NAHUM
TO EDOM
OBADIAH
TOBIT
70 YEAR EXILE
EZEKIEL
DANIEL
BARUCH
JUDITH
EZRA — 10
NEHEMIAH — 11
HAGGAI
ZECHARIAH
ESTHER
MALACHI
1 MACCABEES — 12
2 Maccabees
SIRACH
WISDOM
100 YEARS BETWEEN OLD & NEW TESTAMENTS
LUKE — 13
MATTHEW
MARK
JOHN
ACTS — 14
REVELATION

ROMANS
1 CORINTHIANS
2 CORINTHIANS
GALATIANS
EPHESIANS
PHILIPPIANS
COLOSSIANS
1 THESSALONIANS
2 THESSALONIANS
1 TIMOTHY
2 TIMOTHY
TITUS
PHILEMON
HEBREWS
JAMES
1 PETER
2 PETER
1 JOHN
2 JOHN
3 JOHN
JUDE

Key to Period Colors

Early World	Turquoise	The color of the earth viewed from space
Patriarchs	Burgundy	God's blood covenant with Abraham
Egypt and Exodus	Red	The Red Sea
Desert Wanderings	Tan	The color of the desert
Conquest and Judges	Green	The green hills of Canaan
Royal Kingdom	Purple	Royalty
Divided Kingdom	Black	Israel's darkest period
Exile	Baby blue	Judah "singing the blues" in "Baby-lon"
Return	Yellow	Judah returning home to brighter days
Maccabean Revolt	Orange	Fire in the oil lamps in the purified temple
Messianic Fulfillment	Gold	Gifts of the Magi
The Church	White	The spotless Bride of Christ

Outline of Bible Periods

EARLY WORLD (TURQUOISE) CREATION TO 2000 BC
1. Creation   Gen. 1:1-2:4
2. Fall   Gen. 3:1-24
3. Curse and promise (protoevangelium)   Gen. 3:8-24
4. Flood   Gen. 6:1-9:17
5. People scattered at Babel   Gen. 11:1-9

PATRIARCHS (BURGUNDY) 2000-1700 BC
6. God calls Abram out of Ur   Gen. 12:1
7. Melchizedek blesses Abraham   Gen. 14:18-20
8. Sodom and Gomorrah   Gen. 18:16-19:38
9. Binding of Isaac   Gen. 22
10. Covenant with Abraham:
    - 3-fold promise   Gen. 12:1-9
    - 1st covenant (land)   Gen. 15:1-21
    - 2nd covenant (royal dynasty)   Gen. 17:1-11
    - 3rd covenant (world-wide blessing)   Gen. 22:1-19
11. Jacob steals blessing   Gen. 27:1-46
12. Jacob wrestles with God, name changed to Israel   Gen. 32:22-31
13. Joseph sold into slavery   Gen. 37:12-36
14. Jacob's family moves to Egypt   Gen. 46

EGYPT AND EXODUS (RED) 1700-1280 BC
15. 400 years of slavery   Ex. 1:1-22
16. The burning bush   Ex. 3:1-6:30
17. Ten plagues   Ex. 7:1-11:10
18. Exodus/First Passover (1280 BC)   Ex. 12:1-14:31
19. Red Sea   Ex. 13:17-15:21
20. Manna   Ex. 16
21. Covenant with Moses (Mt. Sinai)   Ex. 19:1-31:18
22. Golden calf   Ex. 32:1-35
23. Levitical priesthood   Ex. 32:27-29; Num. 3
24. Tabernacle   Ex. 25-27, 36-38

DESERT WANDERINGS (TAN) 1280-1240 BC
25. 12 spies sent out   Num. 13:1-33
26. Aaron's rod   Num. 17
27. Moses strikes the rock   Num. 20:1-13
28. Bronze serpent   Num. 21:4-9
29. Covenant in Moab   Deut. 29:1-29

CONQUEST AND JUDGES (GREEN) 1240-1050 BC
30. Israel crosses the Jordan   Josh. 1-4
31. Fall of Jericho   Josh. 5:13-6:27
32. Covenant renewal   Josh. 8:30-35
33. Southern campaign   Josh. 9-10
34. Northern campaign   Josh. 11
35. Tribal allotment   Josh. 13-21
36. Israel asks for a king   I Sam. 8:1-22

ROYAL KINGDOM (PURPLE) 1050-930 BC
37. David kills Goliath   I Sam. 17:1-31
38. Covenant with David   II Sam. 7:1-29
39. Ark moved to Jerusalem   II Sam. 6
40. First Temple built (961 BC)   I Kgs. 5:1-8:66

DIVIDED KINGDOM (BLACK) 930-722 BC
41. The Kingdom divides   I Kgs. 12:16-20
42. Jezebel fights Israel   I Ki. 18-21; II Ki. 9
43. Hosea marries a prostitute   Hos. 1-3

EXILE (BABY BLUE) 722-540 BC
44. Israel falls to Assyria (722 BC)   II Kgs. 17:1-41
45. Foreign possession of Samaria   II Kgs 17
46. Image of the five kingdoms   Dan. 2
47. Judah falls to Babylon (587 BC)   II Kgs. 25:1-30
48. First Temple destroyed (587 BC)   II Kgs. 25:8-17

RETURN (YELLOW) 538-167 BC
49. Zerubbabel rebuilds Temple   Ezra 3:1-6:22
50. Ezra returns and teaches (458 BC)   Ezra 7:1-8:36
51. Esther saves her people   Esther 1:1-10:3
52. Nehemiah returns, rebuilds Jerusalem walls (444 BC)   Neh. 3:1-4:23

MACCABEAN REVOLT (ORANGE) 167 BC-0
53. Antiochus desecrates the Temple (167 BC)   I Macc. 4:43
54. Purification of the Temple (Hanukkah – 164 BC)   I Macc. 4:36-61

MESSIANIC FULFILLMENT (GOLD) 0-33 AD
55. Annunciation   Luke 1:26-38
56. Baptism of Jesus (29 AD)   Luke 3:21-22
57. Sermon on the Mount   Luke 6:20-49
58. Wedding at Cana   John 2:1-12
59. Keys to Peter   Matt. 16:13-20
60. Last Supper   Luke 22:1-38
61. Passion (33 AD)   Luke 22-23
62. Jesus gives his mother to the Church   John 19:25-27
63. Resurrection (33 AD)   Luke 24:1-12
64. Ascension   Luke 24:44-53

CHURCH (WHITE) 33 AD-?
65. Witness in Jerusalem (33-35 AD):   Acts 1:1-8:4
   - Pentecost (33 AD)   Acts 2:1-13
   - Choosing of the Seven (Diaconate)   Acts 6:1-7
   - Stephen martyred   Acts 6:8-7:60
66. Witness in Judea and Samaria (35-45 AD):   Acts 8:5-13:1
   - Saul's conversion   Acts 9
   - Peter's vision   Acts 10
   - Peter's arrest and deliverance   Acts 12
67. Witness to the ends of the earth (45-62 AD):   Acts 13:1-28:31
   - Paul's three missionary journeys (45-58 AD)   –
      - 1st journey   Acts 13:1-14:28
      - 2nd journey   Acts 15:36-18:22
      - 3rd journey   Acts 18:23-21:16
   - Council of Jerusalem (49 AD)   Acts 15
   - John's Apocalypse (68 AD)   Revelation
68. Destruction of Jerusalem Temple (70 AD)   –

YOU'VE TAKEN THE QUICK JOURNEY...
NOW ENTER INTO THE STORY.

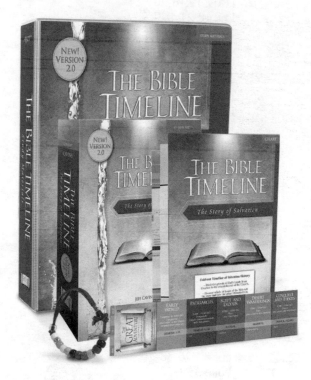

Imprimatur

The Bible Timeline: The Story of Salvation
24-Part Study
By Jeff Cavins, Sarah Christmyer and Tim Gray, Ph.D.

The Bible Timeline is the cornerstone study of *The Great Adventure*. This fascinating series delves deep into the story of the Bible providing you with a rich view of salvation history. See how all of the people, places and events in the Bible unfold to reveal the story of your faith.

Salvation history is covered from its beginning in Genesis through the coming of Christ and the establishment of the Catholic Church.

You Will:

- Learn and practice Catholic principles for studying the Bible.
- Study key Old Testament passages in light of their fulfillment in Christ.
- Discover the relationship between Sacred Scripture and Sacred Tradition.
- Gain a greater appreciation for the Scripture readings you hear in Mass.
- Develop a life-long hunger for knowing God in His word and see how your story fits into "His-story."

What People Are Saying:

"The affect on my parishioners has been wonderful: a deeper love for Christ, a deeper experience with the sacraments, and continued growth and love for the Scriptures."

-Fr. Michael Becker

"I've always called *The Bible Timeline* a gift from God. In one study you can understand so much of salvation history and have the sacraments come alive so strongly. My prayer has been that every Catholic in the country or maybe in the world would do it because I think it would light a fire under this Church."

-Therese Coons

BibleStudyForCatholics.com • 1-800-376-0520

Also Available:
Foundational Studies

Ongoing Studies

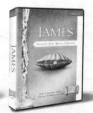

Step 2:
Matthew

Step 3:
Acts

Revelation

First
Corinthians

Exodus

James

Psalms

YOUR GUIDE FOR THE JOURNEY…

This guided journal contains everything you need to complete the 90-day reading plan as outlined in the *Great Adventure Bible Timeline*. It is more than just a journal; it is your personal guide through the story of salvation history.

This valuable guide will assist you with a 90-day plan for reading the fourteen narrative books of the Bible. With plenty of room for notes, this resource contains thought-provoking questions to help jump-start your journaling, tips on how to study the Bible, and a prayer for each day of readings.

The Bible Timeline Guided Journal will:

- Guide your study of the Bible by putting it in the narrative context of salvation history.

- Challenge you with thought-provoking questions.

- Inspire you with insightful commentary.

- Help you properly meditate on the Word of God.

- Provide you with an indispensible tool to actively enter into the story of salvation.

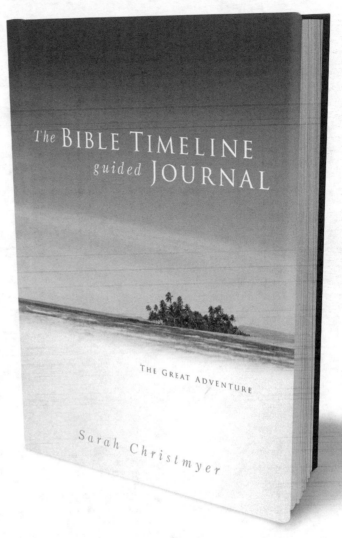

236 pages • $14.95

About the Author:

Sarah Christmyer is an editor of the *Great Adventure Bible Study* series and author of three *Great Adventure* studies: *The Bible Timeline, Matthew,* and *Acts.*